Al-Khemy

or

Being in Two Realms

Alan Richardson

Alan Richardson has been writing weird, winsome and frequently embarrassing books for longer than many of his readers have been alive and is insanely proud of that fact. He has done biographies of such luminaries as Dion Fortune, Aleister Crowley, Christine Hartley, William G. Gray and his own grandfather George M. Richardson M.M. & Bar. Plus novels and novellas that are all set in his local area, along with scripts of same. He has a deep interest in Earth Mysteries, Mythology, Paganism, Celtic lore, Ancient Egypt, jet fighters, army tanks, Wiltshire tea shops, Great British Actors and Newcastle United Football Club. He does not belong to any group or society and does not take pupils because most of the time he hasn't a clue what is going on.

Al-Khemy is another self-indulgent book, independently published.

I don't have a web site, am not on LinkedIn, don't do blogs and am not quite as crabby as my writings might suggest. A more detailed list of my published work can be found somewhere on Amazon Books.

Anyone with a pressing need to contact me can do so via: *alric@blueyonder.co.uk* but please don't attach your manuscripts and ask for 'an honest opinion' because I'm not naturally honest and will always fib.

Some published books

Geordie's War – foreword by Sting
Aleister Crowley and Dion Fortune
The Inner Guide to Egypt *with Billie John*
Priestess - the Life and Magic of Dion Fortune
Magical Gateways
The Magical Kabbalah
The Google Tantra - How I became the first Geordie to raise the Kundalini. *new edition retitled as…*
Sex and Light – how to Google your way to God Hood.
The Old Sod *with Marcus Claridge*
Working with Inner Light *with Jo Clark*
Spirits of the Stones.
Earth God Rising - the Return of the Male Mysteries.
Earth God Risen
Gate of Moon
Dancers to the Gods
Inner Celtia *with David Annwn*
Letters of Light
Me, mySelf and Dion Fortune
Bad Love Days
Short Circuits
The Templar Door
Searching for Sulis (with Margaret Haffenden)
The Quantum Simpleton
The Sea Priest
Dark Magery

Fiction
The Giftie
On Winsley Hill
The Fat Git – the Story of a Merlin
The Great Witch Mum – *illustrated by Caroline Jarosz*
Dark Light – a neo-Templar Time Storm
The Movie Star
Shimmying Hips
du Lac
The Lightbearer
Twisted Light
The Moonchild
The Giftie – in her own words.

To:
Margaret, as ever and always.
Suzanne Ruthven, as always and ever.

And not forgetting my Khem-ical pals:

Billie Walker-John
Judith Page
Laura Jennings-Yorke
Normandi Ellis
Annie Tod
+
my *soror mystica* and best friend
Debbie Marsh

Everything that happens – *everything* – can be seen as a secret dealing between your outermost everyday Self, and your innermost eternal Spirit.

Anon – but possibly Francis X King

The Universe has innumerable 'scripts' for which we provide the actors. Every one of you reading this will at some point re-enact one or more of the great mythic scripts. It does not mean you will become avatars or reincarnations of the figures involved, but 'continuations'. Be whimsical for a moment... Who are you a continuation of?

Alan Richardson, doing homage to Timothy Leary

What a load of shite...

John Robert Maxwell

Table of Contents

Chapter 1

Khem

The Egyptians called their country Khem, or Kemet, literally the 'Black Land' (khem meant 'black' in ancient Egyptian). The name derived from the colour of the rich and fertile black soil which was due to the annual Nile inundation. Khem was therefore the cultivated area along the Nile valley.

8ᵗʰ June 2020

Not long ago, I went to bed at night with the word 'scry' in my head. It wasn't a command from inner sources. The most unlikely things float into my head that have no esoteric value. Only this morning I found myself humming to the kiddies song: *I'm a little teapot short and stout/Here's my handle here's my spout...* My wife Margaret seemed charmed by this and came into the room to demonstrate the actions (which I already knew, I snootily told her), but this is better than her thinking I'm an eejit.

That's a lovely word, *scry*, which means looking into an object such a crystal ball or a mirror or even a still lake in order to see into the otherworld and intraworld - and perhaps the future. I've always envied those who could 'scry'.

Somehow, I've got a photo of the crystal ball used by the legendary Dion Fortune. I've sometimes thought that symbols of things are every bit as important as their actuality, and I've spent light-hearted moments staring into a full-sized version of this photo trying to scry as she must have done with the real thing. I'll probably put a full-sized copy of this into the appendix so you can have a go yourself, by which time I'll remember who sent me this. I actually found that the lights at the 9 o'clock position are reflections of windows in the room where this was taken, and, staring at it long enough I began to create all sorts of fantasies about this place. Is that true scrying? I suppose it is if it's accurate.

I might be misremembering this, but I recall reading something by W.E. Butler (the magicians' magician) in which he described using the blackened inside of a lid from an old tin of Cherry Blossom boot polish to get perfectly adequate results! Can any of my readers remember that product? Does it still exist? I love the thought that while so many earnest scryers are peering into the depths of their crystal balls, Ernest Butler was able to use an old tin lid. Thinking back, I  reckon that the book must have been his best-selling *How to Develop Clairvoyance*. I devoured every word of it when it came out in 1968, practised every technique, but never 'saw' anything.

I've felt compelled to look up the origins of the word 'scry'. Y'see I've got this idea that two essential items for all would-be magicians are an etymological dictionary and – if you're connected to your locality - a book showing the origins of local place names. And even if you're *not* so connected, then the effort alone will pay dividends. In fact I've just received Gary Vasey's excellent yarning book *Chasing the Shaman* that validates that last statement. From being a stranger in a strange land – the Czech Republic – emotionally gutted and spiritually lost, his life began to open up when he sought the Earth Mysteries in a land that until then didn't seem to have *any* and which quickly revealed itself to be bursting with them.

At this time of lock-down because of Covid-19, anyone reading this while living in, perhaps, a small apartment in a megalopolis and yearning to escape to places like Sedona or GlasVegasbury, then you really don't need to. Become aware of the Land, however much it seem to be a Wasteland, and it will become aware of you.

More of that later...

Sorry for the babble. I'm not sure if it's an age thing or a man thing, or just having too many things in my head, bursting out unexpectedly like the sparrows in our eaves. I meant to talk about the etymology of 'scry', so here it is...

The word 'scry' apparently goes back to c.1300 and the word 'descriven', which was probably from the Old French 'descrier', which means 'to publish, proclaim or announce'. Then later in the mid-14th Century it seems to have been used as 'detect, find out, discover' and also 'discover by vision, get sight of.' There are other derivations but I'm happy to cherry-pick this lot and see where I get.

I might have left it at that but the word 'scry' sort of segued into the name 'Sokaris' in the middle of the night, which I haven't had in my head for a *long* time. Sokaris, I would explain, is another name for Osiris, and I wondered if I'd actually been mishearing. When I was at college in Newcastle there was a small group of American exchange students. One wild young lad was known to us Brits as Hurl (rhymes with curl/furl/pearl) because that's how he named himself and that's what we heard. We were all quite surprised when we saw that his name was written as Harold.

So was the word floating in my mind actually Sokaris, and not Scry?

I had to go downstairs at 4 am and track down something I'd written many years ago, for my *Inner Guide to Egypt*. Well, that's a bit of a pose to say 'my' because the scholarly stuff in that was all from my co-writer the late and great Billie Walker- John. From that I learned – or rather was reminded – that the name Sokaris (*sj.k rj* or *sy-k-ri* or yet still *Skr[1]*) was derived from a cry for help that the vanquished Osiris directed to his sisters: 'Come to me quickly!' In hieroglyphs this name was written:

---

1   The Ancient Egyptian language didn't use vowels as we do. Y cn stll ndrstnd.

I'll come back to those sisters later, I think. I don't think they're ever far away from anyone. But I also went on to say:

> It is, really, the cry that we all utter when we are being cut to pieces by fate or circumstance - or enemy action. The nameless, wordless, but utterly impassioned cry into the darkness for help, or succour. It is, in a sense, the cry which Hope makes when it wings out of Pandora's box, trying to make its voice heard over and above the tumult of the pestilence before. It is that spirit of Hope which lies rooted in those immeasurably deep areas of the human spirit. Man will survive anything, will plough through any disasters so long as he at least has hope. With that, he can traverse any darkness, cross any hell.

I don't recall writing that and it sounds a bit over the top to me now. I must have been having a hard time on personal levels. Yet I suppose I shouldn't have been surprised when I got a letter that very morning from the publishers Llewellyn, telling me that this book was

no longer selling, and if I wanted to buy their remaining stock of 40 copies I could.

This is all relevant, I promise.

As I described in *Dark Magery* I had been wrestling with various health problems that had nothing to do with Covid-19, and preceded its appearance by some weeks. In short, I was in a lot of pain and there was a despairing side of me that was really calling out for help on the inner levels. I was deeply frustrated that none of the buggers – of all Traditions - were showing the slightest interest.

Eventually one mid-morning as I lay on the side of the bed in the sun I felt compelled to invoke Horus. I did this both by visualising him next to the bed and laying on his hands, and also by visualising myself *as* Horus and looking down at myself while trying to pump energies into my cells. I'd been doing this intensely for about 15 minutes when...

Margaret came rushing up the stairs to show me the photo she had taken of a hawk perched on our garden gate. She had seen it when she was in the kitchen, and it seemed to be looking at her. She dashed outside with camera and it waited, nonplussed, while she took a couple of pictures before it flew off.

Thank you, Horus, we both said, and while there was no immediate or miraculous cure, I had sense of hopefulness. Looking back M and I both agree that things started to improve for me from then on...

9th June 2020

I'm sitting in the garden office working on this. We've just come back from the local garden centre where we maintained our social distance from the other customers while browsing the plants. M bought a sad, worried looking clematis with a long near-broken stem that no-one else would have taken. I know it's a clematis because a) M told me it was, and b) it had a big label in the pot. Personally, I'd have bought something better, or else snapped that bit off to get it into the car more easily. But when she planted it with its roots in the shade and its head in the sun, next to a wall with a climbing frame for support, I'm *sure* I felt the connection between the two, and relief of the plant itself. The card I picked for her this morning was *The Empress*, and that's

THE EMPRESS.

about right as far as I can see. She is now upstairs in the top room doing her own inner stuff.

Outside the office, our sparrows are going frantic at the feeders. M tells me they've also been having wild sex in the top eaves, but I wouldn't know how they'd even do that. I remember my Mam, the all-powerful Great Mother figure that all the women in Ashington could channel, describing my Dad viciously as 'The most ignorantest

13

man Ah've ivver met!' When I think of how little *I* know about common birds and trees I think I must put myself in that class. We went on a long walk two days ago in the wilder parts of Salisbury Plain (where almost no-one goes) and despite our small handbook about British Trees, I couldn't match any of them.

It was good to get out then, avoiding upsetting anyone still immersed in lock-down, not needing to worry about social distancing in those vast spaces. As I described in my last Magickal semi-Journal, there was a time when I didn't think I'd pull through. Not that I saw any clear white light or had visions of entering tunnels or glimpses of the Angel of Death (who I'm sure will actually be a jolly looking young lady when she does come), but I couldn't see beyond my despondency and pain.

When I did start to improve, after the visit from the Hawk, I determined to get some spiritual healing, and pay for it if necessary. Ideally I'd have liked a hands-on approach from someone I trusted and admired, but in these days of Covid-19 that was never going to happen. Besides, I was reminded of something many years ago when I went for hands-on healing for a relatively minor problem, from a woman recommended to me. She was nice, she did the hands-on thing, but as part of her attunement she had a looped video playing of some particular Guru whom I knew to be what my 'ignorantest' Dad would have called a 'right bliddy cowboy...' or as I would describe him 'a bit of a perv', so the energies she was pumping into me rather stopped dead. I said nothing, paid, her made polite noises and left, with not the slightest improvement.

These days however, it can all be done on-line, and I rather think that looking into the screen of my pc is akin to scrying into a crystal ball and perhaps even more effective than Mr Butler's Cherry Blossom boot polish lid.

So I found a seer, and although I was rather hoping for some direct healing manifesting itself through my earphones, whirling around my pineal and pituitary and surging down my endocrine glands and revitalising their corresponding chakras, it didn't quite work like that.

Somehow, I wasn't surprised that it was (almost) all about Egypt...

You know what it's like when you get a song stuck in your head – an ear-worm. It seems to come from nowhere and plays itself again and again. Well for the previous couple of weeks, after the visit of the Hawk, I'd had a kind of a 'tone' in my mind, although I'm not sure if that's the right term. Not an aural note, not any kind of song, but a sort of *atmosphere* that flowed around and through me. I'm sure everyone gets things like that, perhaps to do with nostalgia, aspirations, wistfulness and all sorts of other subtle energies that can invoke their own 'tones'.

With me, it was all to do with Egypt, or *Khem* as I like to call it when I'm being a bit pretentious. It's not that I keep pictures of Egyptian deities (or any deities) around our house, or even the slightest hint of an ankh. A friend of ours Fran Simpson, sent us a set of tiny pewter figurines of the main ones, and we placed these in various nooks and crannies, but that's about the most you could find. Anyway, to get the point, the seer on the screen (Lynn by name) told me after a lot of previous information about the most ancient days of Egypt:

You will get a Name in the next few days.

She said this three times, and I could almost see her capitalise the 'N' while looking at some spirit to her right. So I guessed that this 'Name' was important. Perhaps far more important than the rest of the reading she had given me. In fact the moment she said this I was already getting a Name, repeating itself like a drum-roll, burrowing into my psyche like an ear-worm.

I'm not sure if this was true clairaudience or not, or if I was picking up information from other levels, using talents that I've always felt were beyond me. Y'see I've only twice before in my life had any moments of apparent clairaudience.

The first was when I was 21, on the edge of sleep and miserable as sin in Gloucester. The voice that woke me was in a grating, weirdly metallic tone and not particularly human. It delivered some stupefyingly bad advice that I made no attempt to follow: *Listen to your Mother's voice and guide your Father's footsteps.* Nice sentiments perhaps but this inner being clearly hadn't a clue about my own Mam and Dad and their endless warfare. Even now, nearly 50 years later, I judge the spiritual advice imparted to me then as being both impossible and ridiculous.

The second was more recent when I was in the churchyard of St Mary the Virgin at Limpley Stoke and I happened to say to one of the Templar-ish graves there: *Pax Vobiscum* and was startled and somewhat delighted to 'hear' the response *Et tibi Pax.*[2]

The actual Name that kept repeating itself was *Khasekhemwy, Khasekhemwy, Khasekhemwy,* although there was also an insert into the pauses that seemed to whisper a secondary Name, though not so forcefully – *Sekhemkhet.*

Of course, when the session with the seer ended I went straight onto google and found quite a lot about these two individuals. I'll tell you what I found in due course, but my immediate concern parallels the instructions given to all surgeons before they even take up the scalpel and make their first incision: *First, do no harm.* In this case, the advice I've given to myself and many others over the years of getting information from inner sources is: *First, don't jump to conclusions.*

Were these names being fed to me from inner sources of historical and perhaps exalted provenance? I wish I could give a big Yes! Had I seen these names before in my voracious and prolific reading of all things to do with Khem? Well, possibly. Whipping myself into a lather of honesty I can say that I was never *consciously* aware of these names, as my obsessions were all to do with the era of the Ramesside kings of the 19th and 20th Dynasties (1292–1069 BCE), whereas Khasekhemwy was at the tail end of the little-known 2nd Dynasty, c. 2890 – c. 2686 BCE, a thousand years earlier. So I can say with some degree of truth that these names seem to have come from nowhere.

Of course, bearing in mind the conclusion I warned about, are these two pharaohs:

- Trying to communicate with me?
- Are they pre-incarnations of myself?
- Or were they connected with me somehow in a previous life, perhaps as friends or family?
- Is there something karmic going on?

---

2   Detailed in my book *The Templar Door.*

Well, the second speculation is very flattering, but I'm all too aware of the many sad individuals who have 'remembered' themselves as exalted figures from the past. My old friend Judy Hall regularly worked with people who insisted they had been Judas Iscariot, Mary Magdalen, Napoleon - and a veritable host of others. Without scorning them, she sought to direct them into looking at what else might be going on at inner levels, that is no less wondrous and exciting. Although sometimes, she had to confess, with some of the clients, the only possible explanation is reincarnation.

I will say right now that while I might enjoy the thought of having been an obscure pharaoh from 5000 years ago, and can certainly slap an astral nemyss onto my often monstrous, Pharaonic ego, at the end of the day I will always say *Hmmm....what's all this about.*

And as I sit here now in the setting sun, I figure that I've got to touch upon Khem once more and try to make sense of it all, and hopefully show that this sort of inner journeying can be relevant to everyone, everywhere.

But first I must insert something of a quick apology...

I think that, stylistically, I've shot myself in the foot by publishing four short Magickal Journals at short intervals, to whit:

- *The Templar Door*
- *Searching for Sulis*
- *The Sea Priest*
- *Dark Magery.*

Perhaps I should have waited and created them as a single volume. I say that because in each successive Journal I've had to use phrases like:

- As I said in the first book...
- In the second Journal I commented...
- At risk of repeating myself from the third Journal...
- If you refer back to the last two Journals I explained all this...

17

Had they all been together in one chunky volume I could have made the flow more coherent, I think, and any interested reader wouldn't have had to buy any of the preceding tomes.

On the other hand I was really very ill when working on *Dark Magery* and am of the age when peers regularly disappear into Amenti. So I've felt a certain pressure to get little chunks of my own experiences 'out there' as soon as possible. Hence my chapters are short, my page counts modest, and I charge the minimum price suggested by KDP/Amazon.

Enough said...

Chapter 2

Those mausoleums of inactive masculinity are places for men who prefer armchairs to women.

V.S. Pritchett

10th June 2020

This morning, in our garden, under a pale blue and cloudless sky, we watched a War in Heaven. M was sprawled in the hammock reading a dark Scandi thriller, I sat in the shade of our cherry tree brooding about Khem. I had been prodded inwardly by something that the seer, Lynn, had scryed for me. When she peered into the akashic library she saw a place that had pyramids but wasn't at the Giza plateau. In fact, as she soon as she started scrying, before she even finished the sentence, I got the place-name Sakkara in my head.

Last night, musing on that name, I'd got up at 4.44 am and looked through what I'd written in my *Inner Guide to Egypt* so many years ago, information that was almost forgotten, sealed in the mausoleum of my own memory banks.

Some of it startled me. *Who wrote this?* I wondered, remembering how I used to scribble everything by hand, in large note-books, altering and correcting, again and again, and then pounding it into existence on my old typewriter before posting it off (always first class) to Billie Walker-John, who lived in Wales.

I still had this floating in my mind as I sat in the shade of the tree in the garden when...

There was an incredible explosion of noise. There, directly above us, winging slowly and almost serenely across was a very large bird that was being attacked by what must have been every crow in all the gardens of our street and the parallel street behind, whose gardens adjoin ours. This large avian, with brown feathers and underbelly, didn't seem to fight back; the crows were relentless, forming an actual dark cloud by their numbers, attacking again and again until the intruder slowly flapped and glided its way out of their territory.

I've never seen or heard anything like that before, said M.

Nor had I.

I don't know what sort of bird it was. It was a very large and certainly didn't have the distinctive wings of any kind of hawk. Our *Pocket Guide* seemed to suggest that it must have been a buzzard. Yet buzzards were apparently creatures of woodland and open country – farmland, moorland or heath, according to the guide. What was it doing here, in the middle of a town, directly above our garden?

So was it a manifestation of the death-bird that was Sokar - the deity behind the necropolis of Sakkara, and after whom it may have been named?

I had to look up what Billie and I had written all those years ago...

> Sokaris, who was hailed as 'the great god who came into being in the beginning, he who resteth upon the darkness' can take a variety of forms. He is most usually seen as a man with a falcon head, though this is an altogether more antique creature than the fierce, pitiless bird of Horus. As Lord of the Mysterious Realms, Lord of the Dead and of the Darkness, he is often linked with Set... He is also linked with the Earth-god, Geb, and sometimes even Tern, the Dark Sun...Sometimes he was shown (usually on coffins) as a hawk with the Red Crown of Lower Egypt and plumes upon his head, standing on a low pedestal from the front of which projects a serpent.

That gave me a lot to think on, not all of it comfortable. Plus If I can find modern 'continuations' of Gods and Goddesses and Legends among the everyday folk of the town, then the same must hold true for the realms of Nature. Birds can be more than just birds. Cats far more than just everyday felines. A scruffy old black dog owned by the ancient lady in the next street can be Anubis, the Opener of Ways.

However, if that *was* a manifestation of Sokar that flew above us, then I was determined to be on the side of our local crows in this battle, and like to think that they were protecting me. It's not that's there's anything essentially malign about this *neter;* one of the problems of working with Khem is that it has powerful gravities that can hold you down, stop you reaching necessary escape velocities toward other realms.

And in selfish terms there are other things and places and Mysteries I want to explore with M when this lock-down finally ends. I'm determined not to get sucked into Inner Khem at the expense of these.

Whoever or whatever Khasekehmwy and Sekhemkhat were, or are, or will be, and whatever it is they might want, then they are going to have to do what everyone else in the world is doing today: Form an orderly and typically British queue outside the doors of my perception, maintain the spiritual equivalent of social distancing, and wait until I call them in. I won't insist they wear masks, though.

11ᵗʰ June

At 6.00 I took M her coffee in bed and pulled out a tarot card for both of us, to predict what we might experience as a couple today. I got the King of Wands, which I take to mean leadership, vision, big picture, taking control, daring decisions, boldness and optimism for us both. Or perhaps it's an image of a Pharaoh with his *uas* wand? I'll let you know if it's right at the end of the day, if I think on.

I suppose my very ancient pack is also a bit of a useful tool for scrying: it is crammed with images as flat and two dimensional as the photo of Dion Fortune's crystal, as packed with imagery as the screen of the pc or our telly, and it has served me well over the years.

If I pick a card that I don't like then I reject that and demand a better one. I do really think we can – or at least should try to – modify and perhaps re-direct our little daily routes as we go along. (Mind you, M and I did have a little tetch recently about me being in the wrong route coming off the roundabout. Try as I might to argue my case, I eventually had to concede. I'm sure there's an analogy in that too.)

I use the Waite/Smith pack incidentally. It used to be called the Waite/Rider pack, the latter name being the original publishers. But it really should now be called The Waite/Smith pack after Arthur Edward. Waite and the wonderful, elfin, cheeky-looking artist Pamela (Pixie) Colman Smith.

(This pack, I would add, is a work of genius, and I'll include in another appendix an essay about using it on the Kabbalistic Tree of Life – if only to show that all the previous Correspondences devised by Mathers, Crowley, Dion Fortune, Frater Achad and ten thousand others over the century have been wrong – even if they did get them to Work.)

It's mid-morning. I've done all my exercises and had my daily blast of on-line Duo-Lingo to master French. I suppose I can try and scry into Sakkara now that I've set my boundaries as high and as solid as the mighty ythat surrounds it.

I must confess it's a place that has always attracted me more than the Giza plateau. It is in fact a vast and ancient burial ground, serving as the necropolis for the Ancient Egyptian capital that the Greeks would later call Memphis. If you lived in Memphis (more properly known as Men-nefer) then for thousands of years you would want to be buried in Sakkara. It was a prestige thing, like Highgate Cemetery in London, or the Forest Lawn Memorial Park in the Hollywood Hills where the Stars are buried. There are various hieroglyphs for this *Men-nefer* over the millenia, just as there have been various names for London over the same, but the one I like best is the oldest:

I tried to find a hieroglyph for Sakkara itself but I've learned, in the wee small hours, that the people of Khem might not have named this great mausoleum after the funerary god Sokaris, as I (and many others) assumed. It was – possibly - named after a local Berber Tribe called Beni Saqqar. Well, the latter notion doesn't suit me at all, so I won't go with that. Mind you I do have a sympathy with the Berbers because, I was told, they regard the Sun as the source of all their problems; I've never been a sun worshipper. I could probably create another inner story and blame Akhnaton for this, but I'll leave that rant for another day. So, to me, this complex has got Sokaris fluttering all over it. The hieroglyph at the beginning of this chapter, in the oval shape known as a cartouche, is of one of the Pharaohs on the King List found within the complex, and means *nefer ka sokar*, or *The perfect one of the ka of Sokar*.

That'll do for me. I'll come back to all of that in due course and try to take you there and also explain that very important symbol of up-stretched arms, known as *ka*.

I must crash out now and try to have some Sokar-free sleep. Take it from me that these inner energies/entities often don't understand the need for this sort of thing. They can be quite ruthless when they've got agendas of their own. And when you think about it, just because they were figures of substance from 4,000 years ago, doesn't mean they've got doodly-squat to teach us today. After all, if a being from 4,000 in your own future appeared, what useful or purposeful teaching could you give It?

I'm sitting in the garden office typing up my notes and M is outside trimming things with shears. I really should be out there helping her, but she won't hear of it. She's also creating a small 'kitchen garden', or herb garden in some spare space. I'm sure she must have done similar in a past life in a convent or monastery in the Middle Ages. If the lock-down properly ends, we still hope to get to our holiday on the Isle of Wight in early July, where we'll visit the Benedictine Quarr Abbey and listen to monks chanting their plainsong, and burst out crying for no reason that we can easily give.

She notes that the clematis no-one wanted at the garden centre is thriving. It has already put out one tiny little, discreet and still-furled flower and several buds, as if to say: *Look, see what I can do. I wasn't the dud I might have seemed!* I've seen a lot of humans express that very same. I've done the same myself, and I expect everyone reading this can scry into their dead but mummified pasts and want to open their mouths and utter the same.

Sakkara again…

I've always been obsessed with the notion that places are as alive as people. I've never been interested in their star signs, or professions or socio-economic backgrounds; I don't care if they wear Rolex watches and drive Ferraris or else put clips on the ankles of their jeans and ride old bicycles to work in a dead-end job. But I'm always intrigued by where they live now and where they originally came from. And I'm talking about the **Land**, and not whether their home is a country mansion or a small one-bedroom apartment in a large council estate.

The place known as Sakkara is estimated to be 4,700 years old - although there are even some contentious arguments about that. The complex is 4 miles long and 1 mile wide and is surrounded by a continuous wall that is 35 feet high. It was – is! - centred around the Step Pyramid of the mysterious pharaoh Djoser, but now also contains smaller incomplete pyramids and also a number of tombs known as *mastabas* – which is an Arabic word meaning bench.

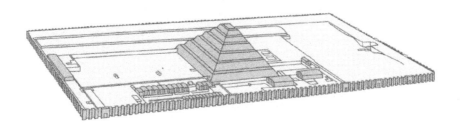

Djoser ruled, as far as anyone can decide, from 2668 – 2649 BCE. His 'Horus Name' as shown below was Netjerikhet which means *Divine of the Body*. Despite his magnificent structure, there has been no sign of his mummy within it, so no-one with orthodox leanings is entirely sure what it was all for.

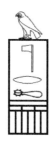

All the commentators about Djoser tend to get over-excited when writing about him and his pyramid, and rightly so, because it was an astonishing achievement:

> Egypt's First Pyramid was a revolutionary structure. It changed ancient Egypt in more ways than one, kick-starting a megalithic construction fever that would remain present in Egypt for thousands of years, reaching its peak with the completion of the Great Pyramid of Khufu around 2,560 BC.[3]

3

It seems to have sprang out of nowhere during the 3rd Dynasty and was remarkable as much for what lay below the ground as above. There are more than 400 rooms below the surface and form what is effectively an underground city. He seems to have been the son and possible successor of Khasekhemwy and queen Nimaathap, but no-one is certain.

Those last words are almost a mantra when it comes to scrying Khem. It doesn't matter whether you are using the sharp and formal tools of the archaeologist or the soft and subtle insights of the seer: 'No one is certain' about anything relating to Khem.

There is a storm beginning outside this little office. M has stopped using her shears. Lightning is predicted by the near-infallible app on her phone.

It'll be good for the garden, she says, wiping down the blades.

I'll close this down and crash out or watch something mindless on the telly – anything but the News, which is all about statues. Oddly, that's the next thing I plan to write about – the statues of the *neters* and the pharaohs.

Earlier, a truly fierce rainstorm smashed against the west windows of our house but we were cozy enough inside. I got on email on my old laptop from my oldest, wildest friend Maxwell. He is, I sometimes suspect, omniscient, and could have scornfully identified the notional Sokaris-bird that flew above our garden at once. I've written about him at length and used him as my foil/fool in my tongue-in-cheek autobiography *Sex and Light,* which is really a love letter to Margaret. I've known him since, at the age of 11 or so, he was regarded as the 'hardest lad in Ashington'. Which, considering this was a place where they played tiggy with hatchets, was quite a soubriquet.

He told me a rather lovely yarn about how, when he was fishing at a particular stretch of the River Wansbeck, a kingfisher perched on the tip of his rod and scryed down into the waters to see the minnows. There's something pure and purifying about that image. More, getting back to Spirit of Place, Maxwell was fishing at the exact stretch of river that connects with the very real wizard Michael Scot [1175 – 1232], who served as science adviser and court astrologer to the Emperor Frederick II and was even given an honoured place in Dante's *Inferno*. Scot was one of the main 'inner contacts' in the Amoun Temple of the Golden Dawn when Christine Hartley and Kim Seymour joined it in the 1940s[4].

Once, in 1990, long before Maxwell conjured up his kingfisher, I had strolled along this same stretch with Michael Scot in one ear and my sister Pat babbling in the other. Scot never 'said' anything that I could put into words, but he was nonetheless an invisible, silent yet subtly communicative presence for a little while.

There is a lineage of magicians within the Golden Dawn who felt that they were reincarnations or descendants of Michael Scot: John William Brodie Innes [1848 – 1923], John Scott, *aka* Lord Eldon [1751 - 1838], Sir Walter Scott [1771-1832], and no doubt numerous others we will never know.

If we can see Michael Scot as being a 'continuation' of anything or anyone from Sakkara, then it has to be the mighty Imhotep, about whom I'll have to yarn later because he is so important.

Pure Shite! – I hear Maxwell's voice in my head, and this is down to gnosis and not clairaudience.

---

4   Track down the now long out of print *Ancient Magick* for details.

Chapter 3[5]

14th June 2020

It is Sunday today and – apparently – Father's Day. I learned that when I went to the local shop to get our papers, all of which are filled with increasingly depressing news[6]. Every Sunday I do the prize-crossword in one of them, seal it into an envelope with a first class stamp (rather than texting the code-word at enormous expense) and fill in the loops of the letters on the address in different colours. I'm convinced that one day someone at that end will see this as an entry from a local idiot, take pity and award me the £1500 prize. So far it hasn't worked.

But I was excited last night, after writing all about Sokar, by the antics of the young pigeon we call Lulu. I'm sure this was the same pigeon that appeared shyly in our long and narrow garden a few days ago and walked and fluttered hesitantly around. She looked at the sparrows gorging on the low table but circled around them, hesitantly, agitating her wings but not daring to leap onto it. Nor did she do more than stare with apparent wonder at the blackbirds splashing madly in the bird-bath.

---

5   Hieroglyph above from the Ka Statue of Djoser, meaning: 'King of Upper and Lower Egypt, Two Ladies, Netjerkhet of gold.'

6   The man in the shop got it wrong: it's not until the 21st June!

Is this how the world works? she seemed to think, before flying off after a long explore.

THE EEJIT

Yesterday evening though Lulu (and I'm convincing myself it was the same bird) was doing bizarre things in the tree: opening her wings wide, turning upside down, exposing herself and twisting into bizarre angles.

Look, I told M, pointing out the window, *She's seeking a mate. That's obviously a mating dance. Listen, that's the pigeon equivalent of the cry of Sokaris... She's saying 'Come to me quickly – you know you want it!'*

M looked and she listened, and I think she might have tutted.

She – if it is a 'she' – is twisting and turning upside down and doing all that to get at the cherries in the tree.

I looked again. M did seem to have a point.

I could spend large portions of the day looking out one of our windows toward the birds in our garden. I suppose this is one reason why I can feel some odd sense of companionship with the statue of Djoser that is sealed in his *serdab*. This is a room set on the northern side of his step pyramid, tilted slightly, but with no door, no means of entry, simply a pair of peepholes that allows him to see out with eyes that were once inlaid with rock crystal. He gazes eternally toward the circumpolar stars. Was he homesick when he had this room created?

There is also a second reason why this *serdab* engages, and although it is utterly ludicrous I must flow with it and tell you about me and my Lancaster bomber...

I got the Airfix model for my 11th birthday, I think. There were three main manufacturers of model kits at the time: *Revell, Airfix* and the oddly named *Frog*. Of the three, Airfix was my favourite because of the highly detailed pilot figures that you could glue into their seats in the cockpit, and finally seal in place with the canopy.

I don't know why these tiny figures were so important to me. I was, you can imagine, outraged when I bought a model from Frog simply because they boasted in large letters on the cover of the box that they were 'Accurate down to the last button on the pilot's jacket'. I spent all my pocket money on that kit only to find that their pilot was a blobby mass with no details at all, scarcely defined limbs, much less the 'last button' on his jacket. I sent Frog a stinging letter but heard nothing back. This was decades before the Trade Descriptions Act came into force. In fact when it did, that blob of a pilot was the first thing I thought of.

I babble, but bear with me…

When I got the model of the iconic Lancaster bomber I was thrilled that not only did it have figures of a pilot *and* co-pilot, but there was also the figure of a navigator, who was given a table and seat in the middle of the fuselage. When you glued the two halves of the aeroplane together there is no way that you would ever see the little plastic fella again, yet somehow, just knowing he was in there, unseen, forgotten by all but me, gave this structure huge power in my mind. It was like having a wand.

So when I first learned of Djoser sealed in his serdab, I think I felt something of awe that one imagines the ordinary folk of Khem felt for their unseen and unseeable pharaoh who was yet physically watching over the realms and peoples of Lower and Upper Egypt for millions and millions of years.

Perhaps, when I was gluing the navigator in place with the feeling that I was performing some small but magickal act, a part of me was remembering Djoser in his *serdab.*

Forgive me for all that.

That battered figure of Djoser is known as his Ka Statue, and he was a powerful looking man with the air of a light-heavyweight boxer.

The people of Khem believed – no, they *knew* – that the soul of the departed was free to roam the earth after death, but that it could use a Ka statue to melt into and thus return home. Someone with Egyptological and/or magickal bent, suggested once that by using these statues as surrogates for actual mummies, the person concerned could avoid reincarnating. I read that a long time ago but never once since and don't know if it's accurate.

Once these statues had been created, they were ceremonially brought to life by priests in a special ritual called the Opening of the Mouth. In the full version of this ceremony, the mouth, eyes, nose, and ears could be touched with ritual implements to give the statue the power of breath, sight, smell, and hearing.

The ritual required the reading of numerous spells, and the sacrifice of a calf. Spells 21, 22 and 23 of the Book of the Dead specifically refer to this ritual. It also involved the use of a number of tools, including an arm shaped incense burner, a serpent headed blade, numerous amulets, an adze and a *peseshkaf.* The *peseshkaf* was a fishtail-shaped knife formed from a wide range of materials (including gold, carnelian, glass, obsidian and flint). It was used during childbirth to cut the umbilical cord. This was a necessary piece of kit as scissors had not been invented.

I think I'm creating a False Memory here from when I was single, many years ago, and Judith Page wanted to perform the Opening of the Mouth ceremony on me. I'm not sure why she wanted that and I can't remember why I turned her down.

I still sometimes wonder what might have happened.

She wouldn't have needed to sacrifice a calf, though...

15ᵗʰ June

The sparrows are making nests *again*. It only seems a few weeks ago that they were doing that, when I was creating the Journal I called *Dark Magery*. We watch them taking all sorts of unlikely materials up to our eaves, and sometimes dropping them because the items are so big. This must be another generation. How often do they breed? How long do they live?

We still watch them obsessively during this time of lock-down. And we will still do so when the lock-down ends. As I'm possibly the 'most ignorantest man' in Wiltshire when it comes to anything relating to the world of Nature, it's an endless marvel to a town-dweller like myself.

Yesterday we saw several little chicks, perched and quivering atop of our Japanese gateway, being fed by their mothers, who dived down onto our feeders and returned again and again to the opening mouths. One mum had a chick on either side of her. And last week a tiny little chick was running around next to our wheely bins. It must have fallen from its nest; its wings couldn't open and just sort of fizzled at its sides. Its legs weren't quite strong enough yet and it kept to falling over and calling to its mum. It kept calling to its mum. Said mum zoomed down again and again to stuff food into the chick's frantically opened mouth. Other than watch out for Schroedinger, next door's arrogant cat who often has staring matches with me, we knew not to try and 'rescue' the chick even though it couldn't fly. But I couldn't resist slowly opening the back door to the outside. The mum was feeding her baby just a few feet away. It looked at me with its right eye and then left, right eye and then left again, and must have decided that I was no threat, or perhaps even the Great Provider, or perhaps even the human equivalent of Amun-Ra, and carried on feeding. I gently scattered some meal-worms before the pair of them and went back inside.

Just as no-one can really understand the vast and ubiquitous hordes of the people of Khem as they've existed through thousands and thousands of year, I don't think I'll ever totally understand the lives of our ubiquity of sparrows, to use their collective name. I've only got to fixate upon the two small flocks in our own top eaves and try to make sense of them, and forget about the greater whole. So I muse:

- Where do the bodies of sparrows go? (We never see any.)
- Do they get mummified by natural causes?
- Do they peer out from under their eave into the circumpolar stars, like Djoser?
- They are offered special foods (by us) in a kind of worship. (We're quite happy to be taken for granted.)

Our eaves are Sakkara, I suppose. Whole generations of sparrows live and die there, and always will unless someone tears off the roof. And those moments when we hear the chicks calling to their mothers, they really *are* calling out *S-K-R*, or *Sokaris*, or 'Come to me quickly!' So of course, thinking about it, everyone reading this will have made the same cry as a baby when they needed feeding or were in distress, which makes us all nascent versions of Osiris in our early days and weeks and months.

33

I've written a bit about the Ka statues of the pharaohs. By an unhappy coincidence the news in this country is all about statues being toppled or defaced or brutally defended by individuals who look even more appalling than (some of) the ones doing the toppling and defacing. There are so many issues here I've never thought about.

I had passed the statue of Edward Colston in Bristol a thousand times, and been to concerts in nearby Colston Hall dozens of times without ever knowing or thinking about his history as a slave trader. I totally support getting rid of that statue.

And then there is the statue of 'Clive of India'. Often known within his own lifetime as Lord Vulture, Robert Clive killed himself in 1774, was buried in secret in an unmarked grave in a night-time ceremony. Samuel Johnson reflected the widespread view as to his motives: Clive 'had acquired his fortune by such crimes that his consciousness of them impelled him to cut his own throat'. Long before he even went to India where he made his name and fortune, he had created havoc and hatred in his native Shropshire. His statue should never have been erected in the first place, and I hope there is no whiff of his Ka attached to it.

And then there was the defacing of Winston Churchill's statue by a young person of colour, writing Churchill 'was a racist.' It made me sad to see the photo of a young man doing that, and I'll tell you why…

When I was in Louisville in 1975 I had a long and lovely chat with an elderly Black (am I still allowed to use that term?) Lo-villian born and bred. When he found out I was English he was thrilled, and yarned about the very happy times he had over there during the War, when he served as a non-combatant in the U.S. Army. It was actually Churchill he praised for allowing him the best time of his life. This is because when Roosevelt organised a million G.I.s to come to Britain and prepare for the Invasion, he insisted to Churchill that the colour-bar should be immediately imposed and rigorously enforced. Churchill, despite desperately needing all the military help he could get from anyone, anywhere, and was in the darkest moments of his Darkest Hour, absolutely refused. So, for the first time Black Americans were able to go to any pub, restaurant, dance hall, theatre or cinema they wanted. They were enormously popular. As one

Englishwoman said of those times: 'Oh we absolutely loved the Americans. They were so polite, kind and funny. It was those rude White boys they brought with them that we couldn't stand.'

So when I see the photo of that young man defacing Churchill's statue I want to point out that, for all his faults, if Churchill hadn't existed then Britain would have surrendered and been immediately Nazified, and that young man's grandparents and great-grandparents would have been dealt with by the truly evil Heinrich Himmler's 'Final Solution'.

I suppose I'm touching here on those issues that have always troubled me: of Goodness that can contain something Bad. Of the Badness that sometimes does Good.

I've got an idea that this is what Khasekhemwy might try and resolve within me in due course, when I let him/it inside my own private *serdab*.

Rant over.

Of course, these statues are soaked through with political rather than magickal energies. Can stones really hold the latter? Can they have consciousness of their own?

Of course! Everything has consciousness. ***Ev-er-y-thing.***

As for stones, one of my favourite yarns (passed on to me by Mike Harris) concerned the extraordinary and astonishingly psychic Canon Anthony Duncan who was, secretly, the senior exorcist for the Church of England. Forgive me if you've already read this in a previous book of mine, but it really is important. Once, when Duncan was stumbling across a Northumbrian moor with a raging toothache he came near a little known standing stone and realised it had healing powers. Upon touching it the pain was reduced enough for him to get home and have it seen to properly by a dentist. Years later, having forgotten all about this small but potent stone, he found himself walking past it again. As he went over to touch it, the stone quite clearly said: 'Is it the tooth again?'

Chapter 4

In the Beginning, there was nothing but the dark waters of Infinite Night. It was out of these that the primordial hill, known as the Benben arose, on top of which stood Atum. The Benben...became a sacred stone in the temple of Ra at Heliopolis. It was the location on which the first rays of the sun fell...The capstone or the tip of the pyramid is also called a *pyramidion*. In ancient Egypt, these were probably gilded so they shone in sunlight.

Modified from Wikipedia

17ᵗʰ June

The first 'sacred' stone I ever tried to find was near Rothbury, in Northumberland, and was marked on the maps, tantalisingly, as *Glitteringstone*. I was going through a kind of internalised madness at the time and fancied that I had discovered a pattern within the Land that resembled one of the cup-and-ring markings that have survived up there. It seemed to me that this was the eastern-most point of a huge, scattered cluster of ancient sites across the county, set in a spiral with its centre at the *Three Kings* standing stones near Cottonhopesburnfoot. These three kings had nothing to do with the Nativity but were known locally as the *Three **Danish** Kings,* who had been killed in some long-forgotten battle.

I found that place easily enough and paid whatever homages I felt due to them at the time, but I never managed to get to Glitteringstone, where I imagined that the rising sun would send beams across the Land as it was said to do from the pyramidions of Khem. I knew nothing about the Benben stone then but perhaps I was scrying reflections of a place – Heliopolis - that was once dominated by a tall, white stone column surmounted by a golden pyramidion that exploded with light when the sun shone upon it.

No-one else in those days (the 1970s) seemed particularly interested in anything other than GlasVegasbury, so I rather gave up my quest for the Glitteringstone after a couple of attempts, and my life went down the tubes then anyway. I have googled it since and even tried to scry down onto it via Google Earth, but there doesn't seem to be any trace of an actual structure, not even a hill-top cairn, and I can't find any explanation as to how this modest hill got its name. If anyone *can* find this out, please do email me. What I have created in my 'neurolithic' psyche is a Virtual Glitteringstone, an Ancient British version of the Benben, catching and reflecting light and creating wonder.

In the prehistoric world they had masses of these potent standing stones that were first cousins to the Benben, large numbers of them still surviving in all sorts of places across the Land. And we have similar in modern Britain with the local war-memorials dedicated to those souls who had sacrificed themselves in wars, for the 'Supreme Good' as they often described it, empowered by annual ceremonies involving wreaths of poppies.

Benben... that was the word that sprang into my mind when M and I panted up the local Picquet Hill to try and find the legendary and darkly sacred 'Bloodstone'. It sprang into my mind because there on the path was a small, isolated chunk of white rock that had the look of a pyramidion – a sort of battered and somewhat deformed but definitely pyramidal shape. I wasn't surprised, because before we set off up the slopes we had asked for a gift of a stone for around our little frog pond, and here it certainly was. I won't show a picture because it came to us privately and shyly, and you have to respect these things.

Now that the lock-down had been at least partially lifted, we were on a Mission to find the Bloodstone, which I knew was in the environs of Edington. This was not so much a 'sacred stone', to my mind, but one that has been misused over many centuries and then neglected.

The lovely, quite beautiful village of Edington, I would explain, was originally known as Ethandune and is regarded as the site of the battle in which King Alfred finally defeated the Danes in 878 and created what would eventually become known as England. In other words, beneath the still and somewhat bucolic surface was more historical slaughter than you could possibly want to scry. Whenever M's many Danish pals visit I usually take them past the place to show where they lost out. They aren't offended. When I was in America, friends there often took me sites where the Redcoats were given a good lickin'. Although, historian manqué that I am, I always pointed out that actually they were Hessian mercenaries, and thus from our second team. They weren't offended either.

But I've always felt very comfortable in Denmark; they always 'get' the English in ways that, for example, Americans don't. (And that's not a dig at my lovely American pals: despite the common language, we have very different mindsets, as Harry and Meghan will be finding out these days.)

So we were determined to find that legendary 'Bloodstone' said to lie near the faery-haunted Luccombe Springs. It's not an actual standing stone, but a large-ish rock attached to a very small barrow. Local tradition has it that if you run around it nine times, backwards, holding your breath, then the devil will appear. Who could resist that! Yet despite our best efforts, we'd never been able to find it. I say 'we' but that was all my fault. It's not marked on any maps and so, relying on my notorious directional intuition, I'd always led us in completely the opposite direction. Sometimes, I've learned, some places just don't want to be found.

Before we set out yesterday, however, I decided to google one last time to see if anything new had been posted about the place, and to my delight found a very long and learned article[7] by one Todd Attebury, who wrote at length about that particular stone, beginning:

---

7   https://www.gothichorrorstories.com/journal/folk-horror-from-wiltshire-the-blood-stone-at-luccombe-spring-starving-out-the-vikings-at-bratton-camp-the-white-horse-of-westbury-and-the-nature-of-folklore/

> I came across a hidden valley and as I walked into it the air changed all around me. There were flashes and sparks of tragedy like nothing I'd ever experienced before.

When he googled the background he found:

> The stone itself is about three feet across, two feet high and a dark, scabby red in colour. It's said that the stone was one of those used by King Alfred's men as a block upon which to behead Danish prisoners of war after the Battle of Ethendune of AD 878, which is how it is supposed to have got its particular shade. There are even paired indentations in the surface of the rock, which look uncannily like the marks left by a pair of front teeth.

Locals who had lived in Edington itself knew nothing about the stone and were no help in directing us. So I contacted Todd via Facebook and he immediately sent me not only a useful map, but the exact Latitude and Longitude of the stone! It amused us both that here was I, living about 8 miles away from the site, and yet there he was directing me from South Illinois, 4004 miles away! He's a nice fella, and I recommend his deliciously weird website.

In that article, written (he later told me) when he was going through similar torments to those I had experienced in searching for the Glitteringstone, Todd went into some detail about the supposed human sacrifices in connection with this lith, but felt these were more to do with the solid power of folklore than the elasticity of hard fact, and from the Romano-British period that was 500 years earlier than the Battle of Ethandune. So probably no Danes involved at all.

I didn't show M the article in case it put her off visiting. I just let her believe it was a small, lost and lonely standing stone, probably calling out *S-K-R, Come to me Quickly!* with its lithic inner voice.

In preparation, I had done a lot magickal visualisation and attempted scrying before what might have been a dark pilgrimage to such a sinister site, and also asked the Land for its permission to visit, giving out a reverse kind of S-K-R in advance – *I'm coming!* - but also asking for any help that might be necessary. There's nothing awesomely magickal involved here. I think that if you visit any new place you should mentally ask the Spirit of Place, the *genius loci,* if you may visit. Visualise them how you will. No need for any bell, book and candley sort of magick. Never leave any litter behind, and be prepared to remove any that you might find.

We had physical Little Adventures on the way and had socially-distanced chats with interesting, solitary walkers atop of Picquet Hill. M did her own inner thing, as always, and I said *Hello* to any spirits in their dark Earthen barrows under the Air and Fire of a clear sky and hot sun. We squinnied down into the 'lost valley' far below that Todd had described, wishing we had binoculars, and it took a little while before we glimpsed a likely-looking rock next to a very small mound. Although I'd been doing my solitary 'Chants to Pan' that are always invigorating in open countryside and woodlands (*Io Pan, Io Pan, Io Pan Pan Pan!*) the direct path down to the stone would have needed the balancing skills of a mountain goat. So we took the long way around, via the sublime Luccombe Springs off the Imber Road.

By the time we got the faery woods of Luccombe Springs, asked their permission to go through their cool Watery shade, and then out into the rather parched valley, I was exhausted but rather pleased. Not too long ago, as described in my journal *Dark Magery,* I had struggled with the after-effects of pneumonia-with-complications, that had nothing to do with Covid-19. I wondered whether I'd quite be up to this trek, but checking the app on my phone, I had now done 63 minutes of Brisk Walking and 140 in total, covering some 5-and-a-bit miles up hill and down dale. And as I made the final stretch toward the Bloodstone I felt that by making this effort and with my own bloods pounding in my head, I'd perhaps proved my worthiness for this particular Quest.

When I finally got there and touched it with my left hand and right brain I was quite moved. I got the immediate sense that its original purpose had nothing to do with executions and resented the whole misuse and abuse. But my first impulse was to go the adjoining small barrow mound and say *Hello* to who built this, for whatever purpose. Some barrow mounds have human remains within, and were clearly used as graves for select individuals, and some don't contain more than, for example, three ears of wheat. I don't know if this one was ever excavated, or what had been found, so if anyone finds out please let me know. But I tried to link with the people who built it in the ancient of days by using a simple technique involving the heart... The one thing that I would have in common with them – whoever they were, and whatever their status – is that they would have known Love: Love for spouse, child, family, tribe, horse. It doesn't matter. It is the one universal energy, if you like, that is also eternal. My simple mantra is: *The people who once built this, knew Love – and so do I.*

It's not the actual words that are important, you understand, but the feeling behind them. And I tried to project toward the mound-builders the sense of: *Well done! You did your best and it is brilliant. This will survive until the End of Days.*

Well, it reads a bit mushy or mawkish, writing it like that, but I can't think of any other way of keeping it simple and keeping it true and smooth. It's the inner *feelings* that are important and not the spoken words. It will be no good repeating this parrot fashion yourself unless you can summon up something from your heart, from the *Ab*, as the people of Khem called it.

As for the Bloodstone I'd brought some water specially to libate it. I use that word 'libate' rather than 'wash' because to libate something is to pour out a liquid in honour of a deity. I visualised any prickly 'attachments' the stone might have accumulated over the millennia as being dissolved. Again, I had the sense that, as far as the stone was concerned, the beheadings it was used for was never remotely its true purpose.

Did I 'see' any tortured earthbound souls hovering around it? Erm… let's say that I created an Imagining. I started by visualising great luminous Gates in the West and told any trapped souls that they can go now, and if they looked toward those Gates they would see the last persons on Earth that they had loved in their lifetimes, waiting joyously for them. *Go to them quickly*, I urged. I did have a brief surge of fear because M was standing directly in the West and I didn't want any tortured Danish souls striding through her psyche. I gestured and she understood, and stepped aside.

And then I went back to the Bloodstone and visualised a line of light connecting from it down into the core of the Earth, and also shooting upward into the Stars.

So mote it be, I might have said, and sat down upon it to rest, because whatever else had been going on, it all felt very right, and that something had been achieved, at some level.

Oh and I should say that I had my *uas* wand with me. All the best pharaohs and *neters* have them, though mine doesn't have an entwined serpent like the one in the illustration. It's actually a 'livewood' wand.

This was given to me by the enchanting, one-off wildwood shaman Dusty Miller in, I think, 1987, along with a small 'palm wand' that we always keep in our car. Both contain the spirits of a dryad sealed

42

willingly within, and as M will tell you they have 'come to us quickly' on countless occasions over the years. You can just see me holding it here, and I don't feel the urge to expose it any more than that.

I learned later that a dozen or so widely-separated and apparently unconnected individuals had, in the previous week, been musing and wondering about the highly obscure and almost unknown Bloodstone. Each one of them had been inspired either to visit or research on-line as much as they could. Who was it who wrote: 'Everything old is a sign of something coming?' It must have been Jung, although it might have been me. As Todd commented: 'Maybe it's calling us home?' - which sort of sends a shiver down my spine, but in a good way.

Perhaps it has been calling out 'Come to me!', like the prone and paralysed Green Man known to the Egyptians as Osiris.

Chapter 5

Ab

When we refer to our hearts in regard to love, or any other emotion, we are invoking a living memory of the ancient Egyptian belief system...The Egyptians believed that the heart, the Ab, rather than the brain, was the source of human wisdom, as well as emotions, memory, the soul and the personality itself. Notions of physiology and disease were all connected in concept to the heart, and it was through the heart that God spoke, giving ancient Egyptians knowledge of God and God's will.

Jimmy Dunn

18ᵗʰ June 2020

It's raining this morning after days of sun and clear skies. *Good for the Gardens* is the invariable English mantra when this happens, and M takes comfort at the thought that the herbs she has planted will now thrive: Thyme, Rosemary, Tarragon, Marjoram, Sage and Oregano. I'm sure she's responding to medieval past-life impulses from some walled and sacred garden somewhere. The lost and lonely clematis she got from the garden centre continues to thrive and prove itself to her.

She's not doing anything witchy with them – at least I don't think so. It's not like she's planting Hemlock, Belladonna, Mandrake or Henbane and all those sinister, poisonous and madness-inducing plants that actually have great healing properties if used properly. On the other hand, she regularly sees the frog who lives in our small pond, and I rarely do. We call the frog Heket, after the Egyptian frog goddess who was said to have breathed life into the new body of Horus at birth and was associated

with the flooding of the Nile and the germination of corn. Women who acted as midwives often called themselves *Servants of Heket*, and that neter is often depicted as a frog sitting on a lotus. Well, we haven't got a lotus in our very small pond but we do have a lily, on which M has seen Heket sitting.

A lot of the neo-Wiccans have tried to link Heket with Hecate and I'd like to go along with them, but they tend to draw the fire of angry scholars. Much as I like Hecate and all her Brythonic equivalents, and often as I've done simple magick at local crossroads, particularly where Three Roads Meet, I'll leave the deeper Mysteries of our Frog Pond for M to deal with.

The little creature is symbolic of:

- Cleansing
- Renewal, rebirth
- Fertility, abundance
- Transformation, metamorphosis
- Life mysteries and ancient wisd

Apparently, frogs can symbolise the need to enhance your intuition and strengthen your connection with the spirit world. So when frogs appear it is time to follow your instincts and trust your gut feelings on all matters.

I try hard to do that. M achieves it naturally. I've often whinged about not being able to 'see' except on rare and brief occasions, but the Irish seer called Acushla told me a couple of years ago that what I do have is claircognizance, and I suppose I'll settle for that. Yes, I do sometimes know things. This is not a boast. I don't live easily with this. I'd much rather have clairvoyance.

And I think that Heket might take me into depths I'm not yet ready to scry, if I peer too hard into her waters.

In more Earthy terms Khem, as I've written elsewhere, keen gardeners had seed-beds shaped like Osiris, the Green Man, in order to help their produce grow. M is doing brilliantly by visualising it all, and sending out impulses from her *Ab*.

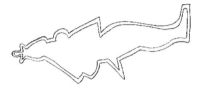

I like the idea of those seed beds. In Britain we have things known as *trugs*, a corruption of *trough*, which do the same thing. M is keen to get one soon, and put it under our kitchen window. Also I must say that I do prefer our own Green Man to the Osirian version. We've got a serious one on our garden wall, almost invisible behind the foliage, and very happy to be in that state.

Although this book is being called *Khem* you won't find even so much as an ankh or any overtly 'occult' symbol in our house, not even in the Upper Room. It's all inside us.

Despite the rain the sparrows are smashing themselves into the feeders, and they don't seem troubled by the distant rumbles of thunder. I've learned that before they die they take themselves to a comfortable place where they won't get attacked by predators and just... die. So I suppose our eaves must be as packed with their dessicated corpses as Sakkara became with every mummy but that of Djoser himself.

It amazes me to watch how the sparrows get up the three steps from our yard into our garden. They give single hops without a single wing-assisted flutter. Those tiny needle-thin legs enable them to hop 3 times their own height like those 'Spring-heeled Jacks' that so terrified the readers of Victorian pulp-fiction. That's equivalent to me leaping straight upward nearly 20 feet. Apparently they have sparrows in Egypt that are almost identical to the British ones, but it's far too hot for me over there. If I did ever have a past life in Khem then I must have suffered badly from the Sun, or else fell foul of The Criminal Formerly Known as Akhnaton.

I definitely want to be reborn as a sparrow on the holy island of Lismore, in the Hebrides.[8]

Talking of which, I had a strange dream last night that was nothing to do with the Bloodstone or Khem or anything that has occupied my mind recently. As I've always insisted, I don't put much stake in dreams and can usually tell where every aspect of the story-line came from. But I do occasionally get one that wakes me and makes me give vent to my favourite esoteric sonic of: *Hmmm...* I dreamt last night that my dearest, tragic Best Friend Forever, Mary Jack, had reincarnated recently as a girl. Mary was marvellous, fun, wild, infuriating, loyal, non-judgemental, kind, and deeply tortured. She took her own life after her son, Angus, took his. We were never lovers, never even

---

8   See *Dark Magery* for an explanation.

romantically entangled, but I still miss her. So I'll be watching out for Signs and Synchronicities and Symbols that this might come to pass.

Which makes me wonder about Messrs Khasekhemwy and Sekhemkhet. I still won't let them into my psyche, not yet, but I'm wondering if they're putting out feelers about reincarnation, and trying to ask: *What's it like out there?*

And maybe souls connected with Bloodstone are doing similar?

I've sent a stinging email to Trowbridge Library. Following government advice it is still closed. Yet following the *same* government advice the local bookshops have opened. So what's the difference? I asked. Trowbridge's excellent library with cafe and restaurant, children's play areas and many computers for public use is a vital public service and far more accessible to me than trying to scry into the Akashic Records.

I await their reply.

I suppose, during this lockdown we are all sealed into our personal, psychological *serdabs;* unable to touch anyone; observing the world through narrow apertures.

When the volcano of Thera exploded in 1600 BCE, on the island now known as Santorini, it undoubtedly caused all the Plagues described in that dreadful tome known as the Old Testament, as many writers have detailed. I suppose the surviving people of Khem then must have known the frustrations of our present Covid-19 plague but magnified a thousand times.

19th June 2020

More rain. Am frustrated that I can't get my Brisk Walking in, except in front of the telly via various Virtual Strolls. It's not the same, obviously, despite the magnificence of the 2-D scenery. As someone who doesn't meditate (coz it never works for me) these strolls are my equivalent.

Plus I like getting out into that metaphoric realm of Heroes and Legends that I've envisioned in the streets. Remember what I said earlier about the Universe operating via 'scripts'. And we are all players in these scripts, everyone of us a 'continuation'. When I pass by these figures from Myth and History I'm not being snide, sneering or ironic. I glimpse them with respect and loving-kindness. The beggar on the street is a continuation of the Buddha. That woman we met coming down from Solsbury Hill as I described in *Searching for Sulis* was a cheery and very attractive Whore of Babylon, exercising her black dog amid the 7 Hills of Bath. When the postman comes today, bringing a book I ordered weeks ago, it is surely Hermes, and I expect that the rain bouncing off his booted ankles will look like small wings. And the guy who challenges people at the entrance to Asda is either Horatius at the Pons Sublicius, or sometimes Lieutenant-Colonel James MacDonell, who held the Gates of Hougoumont during the Battle of Waterloo.

I know that I'm creating a harmless inner landscape for myself, well within my limits of sane and normal behaviour, and you can do similar wherever you live. Expand your *Ab*. Life in the *serdab* need not be boring.

Actually, I did this in a small way with Dolores Ashcroft many many years ago when she visited me in Bradford on Avon. After visiting the small and somewhat haunted Saxon Church, we saw a large and somewhat luxuriant elderly woman walking her dog near the river.

That's 'Dion Fortune' said Dolores, and I knew exactly what she meant, and we both agreed.

Of course it wasn't Dion Fortune in any physical or reincarnatory sense, as the actual woman had died in 1946, and this was around 1982. But she was a clear 'continuation', although I didn't think of that term then.

Actually, much later in the day, I was in The Swan Hotel having a pot of tea by myself and said continuation came in ordered a *very* large gin. 'Weddings', she muttered to anyone who was listening. 'I'm here for a bloody wedding. Weddings always always *always* cause trouble, somehow and somewhere to someone...'

How right she was. I've quoted her often since.

I'm writing this in the garden office while M Skypes a client in Brussels. There are two pigeons on the fence and they seem to be in a mating dance – or one of them is trying. M reckons that it's the *male* pigeon who goes through the motions, puffing out his chest, making cooing noises, giving silly little dances and then waiting for the woman to respond. These two, I believe, are the pigeons we call El Chapo and Lulu. Well, El Chapo was doing his manly best, giving it his best moves, but Lulu simnply pecked him six times on his head and flew away.

If pigeon faces can express embarrassment and disappointment, El Chapo's did so then.

And then... he's pecking around disconsolately in our yard, wondering what he's done wrong, and Lulu flies down out of nowhere and pecks his head again and again, so he flutters off in pain.

And *then*... he's brooding atop of the Japanese Gate, watching the sparrows having fun on the dangling feeders and probably hoping to find some mirror that he can scry into and see if there's something wrong with his manner or appearance.

And then *again*, that cow Lulu appears once more, gives him *another* pecking, even harder this time, wings a-fluttering and hissing, and so he flies off to the next garden to look for someone less nasty and/or more interested.

From being a young bird who recently asked: *Is this how the world works?* - Lulu has certainly learned fast. I know I'm reading an awful lot into this interplay and trying to find metaphors and deep esoteric symbolism. But...

I've been El Chapo.

I've never done a Lulu.

I'm not sure this will help me after death in the Judgement Halls of Osiris. When Anubis hands over the heart of my soul to Thoth, that *neter* then places it on a great golden scale to be balanced against the white feather of Truth, of the goddess Ma'at, on the other side. If my soul's heart is lighter than the feather then I've got a sporting chance of being allowed to pass onward to the bliss of the Field of Reeds.

Personally, I don't want any of that Judgement Hall or Field of Reeds malarky. As far as I believe, here and now as a Brit, I will hang around the earth plane for a little while in my *ka* body to see who is sad and who isn't (making an astral note of the latter). Then I'll enter a self-visualised and self-created realm of congenial souls and pretty British scenery, with lush green pastures, rolling hills, crystal clear streams and picture-book explorable villages that I will know aren't real, but are serving a purpose until I can adjust. And then, after a little timeless while, I'll dissolve into the Pure White Light of my Oversoul and become One with Everyone. As for reincarnating after all this, that's already decided... Lismore and the sparrows for me. And M.

Bliss, bliss, bliss.

Well, that's my plan at the moment. To paraphrase that continuation of Dion Fortune I met in The Swan Hotel... 'Bloody deaths. Deaths always always *always* cause trouble, somehow and somewhere to someone.'

Chapter 6

The name Heka is identical with the Egyptian word *ḥk3w* 'magic'. This hieroglyphic spelling includes the symbol for the word *ka*, the ancient Egyptian concept of the vital force.

George Hart

June 21ˢᵗ, 2020

It's the Vernal Equinox today. Dion Fortune wrote somewhere - probably in her beautifully weird autobiography *Psychic Self Defence* - that the weeks approaching this Equinox are difficult ones for occultists, because of the rising and turbulent energies. I can't say I've experienced that this year, except in term of my physical health – but maybe I'm just not her sort of occultist. Although I went to bed last night and slept solidly, M was deeply engaged with the Equinoctial energies, connecting with the group she sometimes Works with in both cyber-space and inner space, scrying into her laptop in the Upper Room.

 I took M her morning coffee and with my left hand and right brain pulled out a single card from the tarot pack, asking Anubis to give a brief summary of what today might bring for her. It was the *10 of Swords*. Although this might seem disturbing imagery I reassured her that it was wholesome and entirely accurate. It meant that all the torments and despair and hurts she had known in her own life before we came together, were behind her and now over. This was neither the beginning of the end, nor the end of the beginning, but in fact the End of the End.

Of course I couldn't leave it like that, so I mentally told the *neter* Anpu, the Opener of the Ways, to stop faffing about and give M some insight as to the next phase, now that this one was dead and dusted.

This next card, will be the Beginning of the Beginning, I assured her, hoping to get a good 'un, and then pulled out *The Sun*.

That one was perfect. There was the Sun itself, which she loves in ways that I don't; sunflowers, which we both adore (our street every year has a contest to see who can grow the tallest); the white horse that is an image of the local 'Westbury White Horse' carved on the chalk hillside of 'our' kingdom; and her own inner self as a child-like but never childish mite almost dancing with joy.

There's certainly a lot going on today, at all levels, for everyone. Apparently there's a rare annular eclipse in which the Moon passes directly in front of the Sun and turns it into a 'ring of fire'. We won't see it unless we can get to the Pacific Ocean, but just to know it is happening is good.

And it really is Father's Day today. My four daughters, all of whom I love equally and unto death, and whom I've always tried to treat exactly the same without preference (because I have none) - all see me differently as they peer through my Dadly persona into my *serdab*.

I suppose I'm like the Bloodstone. At this moment I've learned that numerous people have visited it recently, some of them because of my posting on Facebook, others (quite unconnected with me), having felt compelled to go there. I daresay that, like my daughters, they all did their own differing types of magick on meeting it, and they will have differing ideas and visions as to what it's *really* about.

At least it is wanted, and maybe even loved again.

22ⁿᵈ June 2020

A glorious morning again. As I whizzed into town to get my Brisk Walking done I was pleased to see two swans and five cygnets at the town bridge. I've never seeen any there before, although they're quite common in nearby Bradford on Avon.

The swan as a spirit animal can help you see into the future and develop your own intuitive abilities...[It] is a symbol of purity, beauty, grace, love and elegance, but it can also symbolise divination and balance. The swan as a totem animal can also help you understand better spiritual evolution and maintain grace in the communication with other people.[9]

I'll have all of that, thank you.

I think I missed a chance when we climbed Picquet's Hill, to do some simple magick involving the Ka Posture. This would have got the *Ab* going too, and by that I mean the spiritual aspect of the actual muscle. I'm not sure if the mystics and seers of Old Khem had any equivalents of the 7 chakras we all now take for granted. I hope they didn't. I find it tedious when we assume that certain aspects of occult anatomy are unarguable and cast in concrete as solid as the pharaohs' statues. I like R.J. Stewart's simple yet profoundly workable system of Earth (feet), Moon (groin), Sun (heart), Star (head), though I don't use it myself.

I speculated ages ago that instead of trying to equate the Mystery Centres of Khem with the chakras, we might try matching them with the pituitary bodies, and so came up with this. I still think it's valid, and so if we're

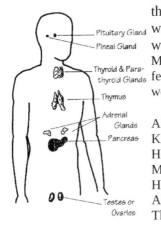

working with the region of the *Ab*, then we're back again to energising Memphis/Men-nefer, which was the sort of feeder town into Sakkara when their lives were dead and done.

Alexandria	pituitary
Khebit	pineal
Heliopolis (Aunu)	thyroid
Memphis (Men-nefer)	thymus
Hermopolis (Khemnu)	adrenals
Abydos (Abtu)	pancreas
Thebes (Uas)	testes/ovaries

---

9   https://dreamingandsleeping.com/swan-spirit-animal-symbolism-and-meaning/

Of course you don't need to accept any of this or even understand it, though you might try to do similar with your locality. You'd need to research what the pituitary bodies actually do and decide what Places in your Land might match these actual qualities. You don't have to make them linear like the chakras: look for Spirals working magickally around you. It doesn't matter if it doesn't make sense to anyone else. It is the **effort** that makes it come alive. Maybe this is the metaphor of the Glitteringstone.

Actually, I was told by a doctor – a surgeon – that my ideas about these pituitary bodies (he didn't use the term 'gland') were pretty accurate, and he took our *Inner Guide* all around Egypt doing his own personal magick in the light of the above. Then he left his wife of many years and went off to live with a much younger woman in Shropshire. He's dead now too...

I babble. I suppose it's my Inner Nile rising and flooding my everyday thoughts, so I'll have to watch that. I was actually trying to get back to the *should-have done* on Picquet's Hill...

You know what I mean by the *should-have-dones* in your own lives: The: *might-have-beens/could have dones/would have dones* and all the attendant *if onlys* that buzz around these corpses like flies, that we can torture ourselves with. I get real inundations of those from time to time, but I'm not sure if they're inspired by the heliacal rising of Sirius, as is the Nile.

My very small *should have done* is presently connected with that trip we made up Picquet Hill, and I will certainly be able to make amends in due course, if the weather stays fine, and do some simple magick using the Ka Posture.

The very first time I saw the word Ka was in the title of a novel by Dennis Wheatley called *The Ka of Gifford Hillary*. I remember it being an utterly boring book, and not in the same league as *The Devil Rides Out*, or *They Used Dark Forces*. But the title has remained in my head, even though I've had to google Amazon to see what it was all about:

With Sir Gifford Hillary and Wing Commander Johnny Norton involved in plans to counter the might of Soviet Russia, interest soon centres on the evil Lady Ankaret and the tragedy which occurred at Longshot Hall, South Hampshire, on the night of the 9th September. A victim is struck down, and from that moment onwards the events which follow seem, at first, fantastic and unbelievable–but are later realised to be entirely logical. What does happen after death? And why should Sir Gifford find himself in prison, on trial for his life?

I've not the slightest desire to re-read any of Wheatley's books now and whenever I see the name I'm back in Bill Gray's house in Cheltenham and he's leading the conversation around so he can say to his wife Bobbie (which he must have done a hundred times): 'Didn't you know Dennis Wheatley was a little shit?' It's not that Bill was involved in any thing magickal (or magical) with Wheatley, but he knew him because of their mutual involvement during the War with British Intelligence – about which Bill would say nothing.

So when I came to see the word *Ka* in later writings, I was already up and running with the basic notions, and that Hieroglyph at the head of this chapter contains the *Ka* symbol, showing it is vital to the *Heka*, the magick.

Remember what I said about the Ka Statues of the pharaohs?  They really were of the utmost importance in that realm. One of the pharaohs made absolutely sure that people would understand his Monument for Eternity by making it with the actual symbol for Ka coming out  the top of his head. I do think that might be a bit over the top, and I suspect this fella might be the sort you would see down your local pub being very loud and muscly while wearing a Superman t-shirt. On the other hand it has done its work by making me want to find out his name, and so it will be uttered in my little garden office 3,795 years after his death: **Awibre Hor.** Sometimes known as King Hor. He reigned very briefly from c. 1777 BCE until

1775 BCE, and although very little survived from his reign this very rare life-sized wooden statue did, along with a fine collection of Wands.

You can practise now, what I plan to do soon and have done very many times before: Assume the Ka Posture.

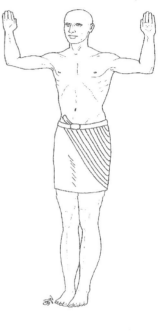

Let's do it Virtually. That is, as I describe the technique in my mind and 'see' it as taking place at a particular site in Wiltshire, become part of it, within me.

There is nothing special about Picquet Hill that I'm aware of, except it has two small bowl barrows and a rare saucer barrow. It also goes by the spelling of Picket. It's not very high and it's not hard to climb, though the road to get near it is not easily found. I've tried to find the etymology of the name using my very old tome *Wiltshire Place Names* but that offers nothing useful. There are only a handful of photos of the hill on Google Images and – bizarrely - one has a fella (not me!) doing the Ka Posture, but out of a surge of joy rather than upwelling *Heka*.

Remember that any hill in your area can be Picquet Hill, and it will be just as potent and luminous as the one I visited. And if you don't have any hill around, or can't easily get out of your apartment, then come into my head for a bit…

You have to start with the 7 Directions I wrote about in *Dark Magery*, but which should be evident to anyone reading this. So…

- **North**, and the sense of Earth, and know that some distance away is the rather lovely small town of Malmesbury, with its Abbey Gardens, that was once a monastery famed for its *Learning* in the 12th Century, and also holds the bones of Æthelstan, first king of all England who was buried there when he died in 939.

- **South** is behind me, with the *Light* of the Sun and Fire at my back, I know that a similar distance away is the town of Shaftesbury, where a Benedictine nunnery as founded in 888 by King Alfred, who appointed his daughter Ethelgifu as the first abbess.

- **East** makes me aware of of the great megalithic structures of Silbury Hill and Avebury and the West Kennet Long Barrow that still thrum with its Airy and omnipresent magickal *Life* – or *Heka*.

- **West,** and I can sense the promontory of Brean Down pushing out into the sea, and all the Atlantean energies of Water – real or psuedo – that were once invoked by Dion Fortune in that *Love* story she named 'The Sea Priestess'.

- **Below** me, I visualise a line of light shooting down into the very core of the Earth, and see its molten and terrifying energies. And from there the line shoots back up and through me, up my spine to...

- **Above** me and into the heavens, into the oldest night of Space, where it connects with a Star that is fundamentally my true Home. And then...

- **Within** me, I visualise the *Ab,* and hear its beating.

I tried to add the alchemical symbols for the Elements which can act like a kind of short-hand when you need it. You might want to look these up. Bear in mind that the very word 'alchemy' is said to derive from 'of Khemia', which effectively means that the art came from 'Out of Egypt'.

When you get confident you can add to the Quarters any of the *neters* that you think appropriate. For example, I once used Geb, the Earth God in the north; Shu and Tefnut (Air and Moisture) in East and West respectively, with Nu, necessarily in the South - although I had some difficulty in making her stay there. Nevertheless the effort alone repaid me, although I wouldn't use them now. You can and should sort out your own Quaternaries, although it's not wise to mix up *neters* from Aunu, say, with those of the Ogdoad from Hermopolis. Once you learn more about all of them from Khem, you'll realise that it would be like plucking four random deities from widely differing Traditions, creating a circle-cross including, say, Thor, Nimue, Hera and Govannon. You might create a temporary European Inner Union within your mind but it will – I promise – soon fall apart.

They who have ears to hear, let them do so...

Even without doing this inner stuff, just assuming the Ka Posture is universal. In fact when I was walking into town recently I saw a number of people using a tilted-forward version of the Ka to 'near-embrace' old acquaintances they haven't seen since lockdown, without actually making contact. One of them – it might have been me – even said 'Astral hugs!' before moving on.

And when you think about it, the Ka Posture can express rage or victory, supplication or surrender. Sportsmen constantly and unconsciously use this when they have won their event, and are exulting. Soldiers will use this when surrendering. Someone who has won the Lottery might glance upward and fling his arms likewise into the Ka Posture to give thanks to Unseen Powers.

So what you might try now is simply stand and go through a variety of emotions while doing your best to arouse them: triumph or delight, pleading, yearning, or perhaps even holy submission to a greater Will than yours. Great actors and magicians do this sort of thing all the time, for the two crafts are closely linked.

Try and do it as I have done – or rather intend to do soon – with your own home town. Extend the vision-lines as far as you need to get in the histories. You might think your town to be little more than an urban Wasteland, but you'll be surprised by what this simple exercise can achieve.

Chapter 7

The ancient Egyptians' attitude towards death was influenced by their belief in immortality. They regarded death as a temporary interruption, rather than the cessation of life. The hieroglyph above is a kind of shorthand that means 'Living Forever'.

24th June 2020

The sun is blistering today, and according to the newspaper Wiltshire is actually hotter than Cairo. Because of the lock-down all the barber shops are still closed so M cut my hair while I sat in the yard. I asked her to make it like Kurt Russell's butch haircut in *Stargate* that I watched last night, but despite all her nifty wrist work with the clippers it's more like Russell Crowe in *Gladiator*. Still pretty good though, and I wouldn't want to meet me in a dark alley.

I noticed the clump of silver-grey locks on the paving slabs and intend to leave them so that one of the sparrows might use some of it for a new nest. Apparently most birds lay two or three clutches, but in a good year four attempts are not uncommon. I think this will be a good year, and they will have as much of my hair as they might need.

I have done no Inner Work yet, and simply slump in the shade, but I can't help remembering that last time I went to Cairo and tried to find the site of *Aunu* aka Heliopolis which, even then in the late 70s, I thought might have been my inner *alma mater*. All that remains now is a single obelisk from the temple of Atum-Ra that had been erected in Dynasty XII and I can't tell you how depressing the area around it was. *Never again* I vowed, sweating obscenely and deeply troubled, as if I'd suddenly been expelled from a place I had loved. I didn't realise then that I'd find the inner essence of the place many years later in the heart of the English countryside. And the Californian Billie Walker-John, as I later learned, had had much the same experience as me, and found her Inner Khem while living in South Wales.

25ᵗʰ June

It's 6 am. After a poor night of sleep because of the heat, I'm now sitting in the coolth of the garden office with the windows open, transcribing my notes, and also trying to work out how to do a watermark for the opening page of each chapter. I say that because I've just made my third attempt over several years to read Tobias Churton's awesome, brilliant, scholarly and largely unreadable book *Occult Paris.* I noticed that he began each chapter with an attractive watermark of faint and spectral figures, and I want to achieve the same for this. I've been fiddling about with the King List that was found in Sakkara. This was of supreme importance to the people of Khem because it showed their lineage and gave actual names to ponder. This is no different to the many people (usually middle-aged and upward) who cluster in the local library and go on-line to track down their family trees. The King List emphasised celebrated ancestors in Lower Egypt and listed 58 kings in two rows of 29 kings each, in reverse chronological order. It started with Ramesses II, and went backward backwards to Men-kau-hor, who was the seventh ruler of the Fifth Dynasty, *circa* 2399-2390 BCE. It seems that it was never meant to be a complete and chronological list, and this was made apparent by the exclusion of Hatshepsut (of whom Tina Turner believed herself to be a reincarnation) and the heretic Akhnaton and his son Tutankhamun. I'll come back to the last two later.

The metaphor behind me trying to use a watermark is because over the past few books that I've been writing up as Magickal Journals, starting with *The Templar Door* and through to *Dark Magery,* I've had to repeatedly mention several important techniques and notions. Such as, for example, my not-entirely tongue-in-cheek use of the Magickal Motto K.I.S.S., and the invariable but simple tables involving the Elements and Vowel Sounds.

I don't want to break off every few paragraphs of this book by cross-referring to what I've already written. The Names, the Elements, the Spirit of Place and Continuations are soaked into every book I write, like the watermarks I'm trying to master, and I'm wondering if I should always put the same Tables of the relevant Correspondences into Appendices in future, so readers don't have to get bored with my O.M.-ish repetition or have to lash out and buy a previous Journal....

To repeat myself even here, The O.M. is not a Hindu sonic, but stands for 'Old Man', although M hates me using this term. Nevertheless, now that I'm retired I've noticed that my male peers don't half bang on about the same stuff, again and again, repeating their stories and often improving on them each time. Fortunately I've a fund of stories – or rather 'yarns' – and can keep this up longer than most, but I do like to achieve a clear and light prosody in my writing.

It's 13.00 and M has just come back from a walk in the woods with her pal Jo, an Edington lass, where they got lost for a time. She is now crashed out on the hammock while I finish off this piece. I'm reminded of Alec Guiness being locked in the tin box in Bridge on the River Kwai, so I'm typing fast to snatch my errants ideas.
I've abandoned any notion of creating a watermark. It...

- Lands in the wrong place on the page.
- Is too bold or too faded.
- Is too small and/or too big.
- It appears on *every* page and so goes on and on, repeating itself like an O.M.

I can create a number of personal metaphors for all of those bullet points. Instead, here is a small copy of the King List below. There are any number of sites on-line where you can see this wonderful piece in detail, along with translations...

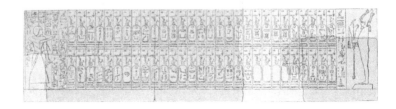

26ᵗʰ June

Last night, on the Feast Day of St Moluag, we lit a candle to the memory of the energy/being who seemed to enter my psyche and our house when I was writing *The Sea Priest*. His presence was entirely congenial, unlike that of the Templar spirits of previous years who made the whole atmosphere prickly. I slept solidly all night, despite the heat.

Today, however, I need to **yurble**. I put this in bold print now because when M reads the manuscript she will pounce on this word from on high. Having once been an editor at a Dutch publisher she has an eagle's eye for any oddities of spelling.

Yurble is both noun and verb. I coined the term myself. This is the second term I've coined, the first being the rather impressive 'neurolithic pathways of the mind' – which will be self-explanatory for any 'stone seeker'. A yurble is a cross between a yarn and a burble, and I need to have a yurble about Sakkara. Or if not the whole place, at least one teeny-tiny artefact found there in the tomb of Pa-di-Imen and dated to approximately 200 BCE. It is simply a bird-shaped object with a wingspan of 7.1 inches and made from sycamore wood.

I was still trying to find a suitable watermark based on Sakkara when my browsing glimpsed the drawings that numerous people had made of it. At once I was thrown back into the mausoleum of my own memories to the days when I was assembling that model of the Lancaster bomber with its own secret and sealed *serdab* for the its navigator.

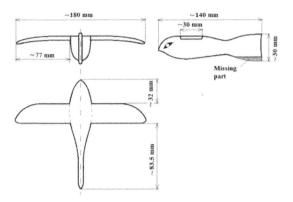

I was bemused by the numerous on-line arguments as to whether this small object could actually glide and also – perhaps – show evidence that the pharaohs had access to advanced technologies. Something that I personally doubt.

But I was remembering when I had made a flat template out of hard balsa wood in an aeroplane shape not too dissimilar to the outline of the Sakkara Bird as it is known. I then cut into it the gently curving slot into which I planned to slide various wing-shapes. Those of you who know their aeroplanes will, of course, know all about the Bernoulli's principle which makes actual heavier-than-air flight possible.

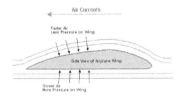

Using stiff cardboard I experimented with a variety of wing-shapes, through straight, swept and different deltas, flinging my craft across the sitting room and making notes of its flight. And then, out of sheer curiosity, I fitted a completely circular wing of the sort you'd never see in a real aeroplane. When I launched it across the room toward my plastic model of the Cutty Sark, it flew beautifully, but with a rising and falling flight path.

I was immediately reminded of Kenneth Arnold's historical description of the unidentified flying objects he saw in 1947, when he likened their movement to saucers skipping on water.

Hmmm… I thought then.

Hmmm… I think now as I look at the Sakkara Bird.

Am I yurbling that this simple model has something to do with ET's? Not at all. I'm just saying that the hawk-image from the necropolis resurrected a small memory that flew out of a lost and youthful tomb and into my present life. Mind you, it's M's 60th birthday soon (she only looks about 45) and because I always make her things, I wonder if she'd like her own Sakkara Bird to throw around the garden?

On reflection, I think not...

The postie has just come. He is not Hermes today, but a cross-looking demon from a Very Hot Place. He has delivered the single gratis copy of *The Inner Guide to Egypt* that I requested from Llewellyn when they decided to dump the remaining handful of copies of their print-run. The book is sealed in its waterproof, tamper-proof, vacuum-packed(?) international air-mail envelope. I have no intention of opening it. I will put it in the Upper Room and it will remain there like a mummy in its sarcophagus, pure and untouched for millions and millions of years. For my own records I note that during the 10 years it has been in print it has sold 2,670 copies. It's boon companion in the Llewellyn's range, my own 'best-selling' *Aleister Crowley and Dion Fortune,* has sold 2,989 copies in 11 years.

When I was 20, I was told by Neville Armstrong, the senior editor behind the now-defunct publishers 'Neville Spearman': *Books on Magic don't sell, Alan. I don't know why but they just don't.*

I mention all this because a few years ago a work-mate who found out that I was writer in my spare time made the comment:

Wow, you must be loaded!

I must, I replied, coz I knew he'd never believe me.

Chapter 8

Egyptians believed all they had to do was recognize how the world worked, who was responsible for its operation, and behave accordingly. This behaviour was directed by the central cultural value, *ma'at* (harmony and balance) which was sustained by an underlying force known as *heka* (magic). *Heka...* had been present at the creation of the world, pre-existing the gods, and allowed those gods to perform their duties.

J.J. Mark

27ᵗʰ June

When I took M her morning coffee and did the tarot, I picked out the **5 of Wands** for her. After looking through the various meanings, she decided to accept: 'Some attributions say it is a card of gold, gain and opulence.' The card I picked for myself was the ominous looking **6 of Swords**. *I'm not having that*, I said, and shuffled the pack more vigorously this time, telling the Inners to get a grip. I got the **6 of Swords** *again* so of course I looked more closely at the possible meanings and had a Good Think. In fact the Think was probably perfect: 'Journey by water, route, way, envoy, commissionary, expedient.' Even reversed – which I usually ignore if it doesn't suit me – it read: 'Declaration, confession, publicity.' Well, young  Gary Vasey from the Czech Republic is arranging at this very moment, via emails, to do an interview of me for a pod-cast. And before I even did the tarot reading M and I had been excited by the fact that in one week's time we'd actually be off on our long-booked holiday and 'journey by water' to the Isle of Wight. For several months we'd been worried that the lock-down might still be in place, but it opens up on July 4ᵗʰ, our original date of travel.

The Isle of Wight is one of our favourite holiday destinations, and we can get to the ferry from our place within a couple hours at my snail-pace of driving. And on this trip I'm excited about meeting, for the first time in 47 years, someone who is not only an Old Soul but – I certainly believe – a Great Soul. Though, tough Yorkshireman that he is, he'd laugh his socks off if I ever said that to him.

Which brings me around to the notion of Great Souls and the priesthood in Khem...

The hieroglyph at the beginning of this chapter depicts a *web/wab* priest, and also has the sense of depicting the purity and ritual cleanliness of that caste.

This one is given the tantalising name of Great Seer, and might be pronounced something akin to *uu maa*.

This refers specifically to the Heka Priest

The two letters S and M become the Sem Priest.

This is another name for Priest, meaning literally the Pure One.

This means 'Master of Secrets'.

The *Sem* was one of a number of specialist priests, whose duties involved inducing trance-like states akin to those of modern shamans, wherein visits to the Otherworld were undertaken. For instance, the Sem for Abydos would go into a trance, a 'temple sleep', before the statue of Osiris while enwrapped in a garment that made him strangely reminiscent of a bee. He would go into his 'Horus Sleep' which could take all night, and seek to capture the wandering soul of his father, Osiris, and install it into the statue which was now regarded as having an actual soul, and so fully alive. In the morning, while he was still wrapped in the bee-stripes, he would announce to the jubilant crowd that Asar-Un-nefer, the Green Man and Horned God (all variant titles of Osiris), had triumphed over death once more.

(To be honest, I actually had to refer to *The Inner Guide to Egypt* for that, tearing it out of the 'eternal wrappings' I'd left it sealed in just yesterday. I had forgotten just about all of the preceding except that the symbol of the Bee was profoundly important. You might want to track that book down and take full advantage of Billie's scholarship, rather than the *keep-it-simple* taster I've just given.)

Did the ordinary folk of Khem see much of what the priests did?
    Not much at all.
    The temples of Khem, throughout its long history, weren't like the churches or cathedrals you'd find here in the West. That is, the common people didn't go into a designated space and listen to the priests talking to them and interceding for them, or involving them in any sacred acts like Holy Communion. The priests didn't preach, interpret scripture, proselytize, or conduct weekly services. Their sole responsibility was to care for the god or goddess in the temple. As long as they did, the ordinary people were happy to carry on with their lives knowing that the stars, law, morality, order, harmony, the seasons, and cosmic balance of Ma'at were all being maintained.

> Men and women could be clergy, performed the same functions, and received the same pay. Women were more often priestesses of female deities while men served males, but this was not always the case as evidenced by the priests of the goddess Serket, who were doctors and both female and male, and those of the god Amun.[10]

I quote that above simply because an Adept of my acquaintance won't have it that there were actually priestesses in Khem. Mind you,

---

10 https://www.ancient.eu/article/1026/clergy-priests--priestesses-in-ancient-egypt/

he always bristled at the very notion that the practices in the earliest days of Khem were derived from shamanism, despite the numerous on-line scholarly articles I could send him. He raged at the word 'shaman' like Bill Gray used to rage at the word 'witch'.

Hmmm… the computer just crashed - just after I'd had another whimsical dig at the old rascal I was describing above. Remember in *Windows '98* when you'd regularly get for no reason the dreaded Blue Screen of Death? Well this was, for no reason, the Black Screen of a Miffed Mage.

Okay okay, I'll leave him alone. Glad to see he's still got it – the *Heka*, I mean.

It's tipping down now and I need to get some stuff in town for our holiday. I'll come back to the priesthood of Khem later and discuss whether they've got anything to teach us today.

28ᵗʰ June

I'm in a state of no small excitement because at 6 pm my beloved Newcastle United are playing against Manchester City (in an empty stadium) in the quarter-final of the F.A. Cup. And it's televised. The tarot card I plucked when asking if my team would win was the **Ace of Swords** – which I take as a Yes! The lads will need all the *heka* they can get.[11]

But I suppose it must seem odd that a man like me, from the north-east of England but now totally immersed in the south-west, should be using the symbols and energies and entities from the Middle Eastern realm that I think of as Khem.

That's an easy one to answer…

Let's imagine we're atop of Picquet Hill again, looking northward. From there to Sakkara, as the crow flies eastward, is about 3,589 miles. Yet if I look down from that hill over the green and pleasant English landscape, it is discreetly filled with large numbers of souls who habitually use the symbols and energies and rituals of all that emerged from Bethlehem, which is about 3,720 miles distant – even

---

11   They got totally stuffed.

further away. To those followers, the Mysteries of their Christ are part and parcel of their English landscape.

I'm sure you get what I mean. Khem is a place within. I'm not always going to be visiting it once I release myself from the *serdab*, and confront Messrs Khasekhemwy and Sekhemkhet, but I'll stroll through its by-ways quite happily for the moment...

It's 2 pm and I crashed out in my own equivalent of a Horus Sleep – otherwise known as an Old Man's Nap. Apparently there was an apocalyptic rainstorm but I heard nothing. What woke me were various titles that came fluttering and buzzing into my mind with the sort of hieroglyphs that I could send to the afore-mentioned Adept, showing that notions of priestesses were actually carved into stone.

There was:

          Priestess of Hathor

   Divine Chantress

And the incantatory title: *Mistress of the house, god's servant of Hathor, lady of the sycamore* [ie Hathor], *divine chantress, king's acquaintance* which was shewn as:

And there was also the hieroglyph *ḥm.t nṯr n imn* :

   *God's Wife of Amon*, a priestess role which apparently could become more powerful than that of the King. This was the highest-ranking **priestess** of the Amun cult centred in Thebes, in Upper Egypt, during the Twenty-fifth and Twenty-sixth dynasties.

Do I see myself as some sort of priest and M as a priestess? Well, I wrote a whole book about her being my *shakti*, so I suppose in simple secretive terms, we *are* both priest and priestess. But I maintain that this applies to everyone. We are all priests and priestesses when we make the slightest effort not just to reach *inward*, but when we then, each in our own quiet ways, reach *outward* to help our fellow souls. Without the latter, it's just a kind of pleasurable, spiritual masturbation and shouldn't be touted as anything more than that.

Well that's my opinion at the moment but I think I might be a bit waspish today. Ask me again later.

Another memory – or is it a yurble? – has just floated into my mind and so I'll have to go with it...

Some years ago while sitting in a cafe in GlasVegasbury I listened to a woman on the next table saying that she'd done her week's training, and was now a fully initiated Priestess of Avalon. This was the title with which she would market herself back in the States.

That irritated me then and still does, and I wonder why. Was I – am I – perhaps jealous? Jealous and resentful that I've never been able to make a living writing about magick and practising it every moment of every day? That must play a part. It do sting myself a bit, I suppose. I'm not sure.

The raining is torrential outside the garden office. It is bursting on the pathways into a million coronets. There's a slight sound of distant rolling thunder; I can't help but think about the 'initiated' part also. And now the image of someone I shall call Doris comes in with it, and sort of agitates the air around me.

Doris is now long dead and had once been an initiate of the *Fraternity of the Inner Light,* and close to its legendary founder, Dion Fortune, who died in 1946. I wrote to her asking if she had any memories of DNF, as they tend to call her, and if she could confirm rumours that the latter had been sexually active with both men and women in her last years, making up for lost time. (And I will insist right now that I regard these actions, if true, as positive and healthy and altogether praiseworthy.)

71

I asked Doris that because she herself was known to have been - how shall I say this - a very 'friendly' woman. Indeed throughout the 1950s she was a, enthusiastic visitor to 'Avalon – the wooded place'. Now this was not, as you might suppose, a reference to Chalice Orchard in Glastonbury in that pure era before it was deluged by crystals. 'Avalon' was the name of chalet that the initiates of the FIL maintained throughout that period in Brickett's Wood, which was one of the first nudist camps in Britain.

In the event I got a truly vicious letter in reply, not because I was asking about human, personal and sexual things, but because – in her damning words – I was 'not an Initiate, and so couldn't *possibly* understand *anything* about her old teacher and boon companion!' She then vowed to contact everyone she knew to put them off me, and would do *everything* in her power to spoil my research.

Please understand that she was not in any way upset about my actual questions, but because I was **Not An Initiate!** I might be having a slip in time here, but I remembered an episode from the old film *Charge of the Light Brigade* (or it might be the series *Sharpe*, with Sean Bean) in which the titled English officers of the 1800s were appalled by the presence of an officer who had made his way up the ranks through merit and bravery and was not – horror of horrors – *not* a nobly-born Gentleman of Breeding!

I wrote her a long letter back giving her a list of High Initiates of the past and present who, despite their undoubted ceremonial status as 'Initiates', were in all, human terms, either absolute perverts or truly dreadful individuals. If any of my readers want homework then they should find half a dozen examples of their own to set themselves free from the enduring 'glamour' of Initiates. And put in the middle of them Charles W. Leadbeater, the 'Elder Brother', High Initiate and spurious seer who groomed Annie Besant and would have been arrested today because of his obsession with young boys. (As Krishnamurti said at the end of his life: 'Leadbeater was evil.') I pointed out the various Gurus who were making fortunes in those heady days, all of them buying Rollers with their dosh when they weren't abusing their disciples. I pointed out Heinrich Himmler, the highest Initiate of his own Order within the S.S. that was run from his temple at Wewelsburg. I mentioned the various King and Queen Witches who fibbed about their initiatic origins, whose behaviours were far from supernal, and whose teachings were a stolen mish-mash. I would have mentioned L. Ron Hubbard, an initiate of Crowley's O.T.O., but I didn't, as Doris was living on the Scientology estate at the time. There were more, but I've forgotten.

To be fair, she took my point, I think, and became quite cordial after she had studied my detailed letter, and then told me all she knew – which wasn't much. I think, in other circumstances, I'd have liked her.

Rant over.

The rain has stopped.

Chapter 9

And then there was only the silence of the stars, and space, and blackness and a void which was and is, and is to come, for in the end is also the beginning, and this void, being Nothing, could not be created, and this void, being Nothing, could not be destroyed, and this void being Nothing, is and was and will be, and this void, being Nothing, is not, was not and will not be. It exists and does not exist forever, has existed and has not existed forever, will exist and will not exist forever; no words can describe that Nothing which is perceived and yet not perceived. We are separate from that Nothing, and we judge time as a series of events. Were we One with that Nothing, there could be no Time.

The Devil's Maze, Gerald Suster

July 1st 2020

It's 6.30 am and it's grey and calm outside the garden office, which might mean it's going to be a scorcher again. The blackbird we call Meatloaf is gadding about, totally unmoved by my presence when I go near. As I think I've already said, of course it's *not* the same bird we named Meatloaf when we first observed him some years ago, but we still use the name. There have been any number of Merlins and Arthurs and Morganas, and they're all initiatic titles, used by 'continuations'. So our Meatloaf is no different. Although the one fluttering in the bird bath at the moment is noticeably smaller and slimmer than the blackbird who first serenaded us years ago, it's the same Being.

It's July 1st today and if I'd been living in Khem in the Ancient of Days, I'd be expecting the Inundation. Until they built the Aswan Dam in 1960, the Nile rose and flooded its banks every year between June and September, in a season they called Akhet. It must have been a magickal moment when it rose like the back of a great black serpent and they wouldn't have cared that the flood was actually caused by heavy summer rains in the Ethiopian highlands, swelling the different tributaries and other rivers that joined and became the Nile. To them, this was the coming of the androgynous *neter* Hapi, bringing fertility to the land. This was achieved when the flood decreased in size by September, leaving behind a deposit of rich, black silt on which their crops would thrive.

There's nothing happening like this in the garden at the moment, although we do have the regular occurrences of the Severn Bore not far from us, that I keep meaning to watch. This is a tidal bore formed when the rising tide moves into the funnel-shaped Bristol Channel and Severn Estuary and the surging water forces its way upstream in a series of waves, for some 21 miles. Depending on the strength of the bore, associated with the phases of the Moon, it is possible to surf the entire length. The current record for riding the bore stands at 9.25 miles.

I'm only burbling about that, though, because at the moment I'm feeling a bit flat, a bit dry and a bit uninspired. Perhaps I'm waiting for a tidal bore to come surging up within my imagination. Instead I'm either staring at a blank page in my notebook or the dead screen of my pc and nothing seems to be happening. Not sure if I should try and invoke my inner Hapi. Not sure if he/she is the solution.

A curious thing has just happened… I decided to leave my *serdab* in Sakkara for a little while to try and get inspiration from a Mystery Centre in Hermopolis that was more purely known as Khemnu, and where the *neters* known as the Ogdoad were dominant. These *neters* were grouped into four pairs which carried the titles Night, Obscurity, Secret and Eternity, and usually bore the heads of frogs and serpents. I had a nice little table of correspondences that I cut from my *Inner Guide* and felt it would fit perfectly if I pasted it here. Yet the actual names of the *neters* refused to transfer, and/or the pc kept freezing. I've spent the past half hour cutting and pasting and then typing out their individual names – their *rens* – laboriously, but they refused to make an appearance, and so I must accept this. The most that *They* would allow was this paragraph:

Khemnu is an atmosphere rather than a doctrine. A place where wisdom is attained through inversions, much as Alice found when she stepped through the looking glass. Other recensions were based upon an androgyne deity emerging with a cosmic burst of light and consciousness to take his place upon the land, but Khemnu emphasised the opposite of these qualities. In the crude sense, the priests of Khemnu knew that without darkness we could not appreciate light; without nothingness we could never have somethingness; without not-knowing we could never have true gnosis.

And the most that I could transfer of the table with *Their* names is the one below. If it speaks to you, fill in the columns yourselves. I can't even get it to centre how I want, and believe me when it comes to formatting things like this I'm an Adeptus Major at least, and possibly even a Magister Templi.

Abyss	Hidden Ones	Obscurity	Darkness
Eternity	Secret	Inertness	Nothing
Infinity	Invisibility	Mist	Night
Matter	Energy	Time	Space

The quote at the beginning of the chapter is by Gerald Suster. This is one of those chunks of prose that I wish I had written. It tells a lot of things on several levels, all overlapping, all elegantly construed. I met him in 1986, when he came to visit me at Murhill, at the enchanted cottage described writ large in my novella *The Moonchild*. He was with Laura Jennings, the hierophant of the Ra-Horakhty Temple of the Golden Dawn, from America. Gerald was from what people of our generation still wryly referred to as The Smoke, *aka* London, and as they looked out of the glistening and silver depths of the Limpley Stoke Valley he sighed: *Most of England is like this, Laura...*

Gerald was the same age as me and something of a genius, I think, but also something of a Terrible Warning, as his alcoholism was clearly apparent even during a bucolic moment like this. I don't know if he ever managed to master this illness – for that's what it is – but I was sad when I learned of his death in 2001.

Although the quote is by Gerald Suster I actually saw it in *The Atum-Re Revival*, by the splendidly named Melusine Draco. The book sort of leapt out at me and I grasped it as if I were the goddess Iusaas - which all the Khem-ical cognoscenti will know is actually a bit of a dirty joke on my part. I don't think I'm revealing any hidden secrets when I say that Melusine Draco is another aspect of Suzanne Ruthven. I say 'aspect' rather than pen-name because between them they've written a series of books that are totally different, innovative, learned and challenging in very different Traditions. Most writers have only one string on their literary banjos and they pluck out the same old tunes on the same old topic in the same old way. Melusine Ruthven (or Suzanne Draco) have at least twelve strings they can make extraordinary tunes on.

Some time ago a correspondent warned me that – I use the exact words here – 'Suzanne Ruthven has just boasted that she got Alan Richardson writing again.'

I assured the correspondent that it was not a boast but a simple statement of fact. When my life was at rock bottom and no publisher was showing the slightest interest in me, Suzanne published my tongue-in-cheek and utterly weird autobiography *The Google Tantra – How I Became the first Geordie to Raise the Kundalini*. And also encouraged me to do *The Old Sod*, a biography of William G. Gray that I finished with the help of Marcus Claridge. She did the second edition of our *Inner Guide to Egypt* and she would have done *The Giftie* too, as she was the first to twig that it was meant to be a vehicle for Billy Connolly, but then her lovely little Ignotus Press had a downturn. In fact, more than any other person I know, Suzanne had the ability to scry when I used hidden techniques in my prose to 'send out signals' that others might respond to.

(And as I write this another little bubble emerges from my own far-from-primordial depths and has just popped, leaving me with ego on my face... I was pontificating earlier about initiations and initiators and probably doing my holier-than-thou thing. Yet I've just remembered that I was once asked to go to a certain place in

Leicestershire to help facilitate the initiation of a young woman into a certain group. All I did was radiate some Set energies, but everyone assured me it worked. And – oh gosh – I wore a black robe! For me the most memorable event was that night when I had an intensely lucid dream, in which the female magus of the group came to me and was – how shall I say this? - very friendly. The next day over breakfast the lady in question grinned hugely, knowing exactly what we had done and how much I'd both enjoyed and needed it. Those with ears, let them hear.)

It's Suster's notions of Nothingness that we invariably have to deal with at some point in any Magickal Journey. Whole books have been written about this, some detailing the various Egyptian Creation myths that described how the Universe was created from Absolute Nothingness by a variety of *neters,* and some drawing parallels with modern Big Bang Theories or the primal nil-concept of the *Ain Soph Aur* from the Kabbalah. I don't want to delve or dive too deeply into any of those at the moment., though.

But I also rather like the parallel idea of the Primordial Waters of Nu from which All eventually sprang. I won't try again to type the names of the Ogdoad because they clearly – at this particular moment – don't want to be dragged into the light of my personal day. Perhaps there was some antagonism between Hermopolis and Messrs Khasekhemwy and Sekhemkhet? Perhaps they just don't like *me* at the moment. Even so, I'd be a pretty wimpy pharaoh if I didn't *try* to explain that…

The eight gods were originally divided into male and female groups, and symbolically depicted as aquatic creatures because they dwelt within the water: the males were represented as frogs, and the females were represented as snakes. These two groups eventually converged, resulting in a great upheaval, which produced the pyramidal mound. From it emerged the sun, which rose into the sky to light the world.

There. I dunnit. There's a heavy rain falling outside but it's not a hard rain as far I can tell, and the sky is still in its usual place.

So… the hieroglyph at the beginning of this chapter is that of Nu, or Nun, regarded as perhaps the oldest of the *neters* and father of Re, the sun god. Nun's name actually means 'primeval waters', and he represented the Waters of Chaos out of which Atum-Re began creation. Nun was also thought to continue to exist as the source of the annual flooding of the Nile River. Despite all the various Creation myths that the people of Khem subscribed to, they had one thing in common, Nun. Even though the myths named different gods as the original Creator, they all agreed that he sprang from Nun, the primordial waters. Nun was more than an ocean, he was a limitless expanse of motionless water. Even after the world was created, Nun continued to exist at it's margins and would one day return to destroy it and begin the cycle again.

I like the notion of primeval waters because where I'm writing now was once, 10,000 years ago or less, part of a shallow inland sea. If we could time-travel and stand atop of Picquet Hill again and look northward, it would be a vast area of water broken only by countless small hills. In those waters, you would see ichthyosaurii, basking sharks, dolphins and all manner of aquatic creatures now extinct. In fact, standing atop of any hill in this area it's hard *not* to try and visualise this. 'Believing is seeing, Alan', as Robert John Langdon wrote to tell me in this context after I'd bought his adjusted maps for this area..

This is not the character 'Robert Langdon' from the insanely successful *The Da Vinci Code* by Dan Brown, but a writer of unusual little books with unexpected insights about the Ancient of Days. In 2014 he developed the revolutionary hypothesis that the ancient monuments of Britain and Europe were built on the shorelines of the 'Post Glacial Flooding' that occurred directly after the last Ice Age.

> This discovery has opened the distinct possibility that the 'megalithic builders' of Northern Europe were a single maritime civilisation that used boats to transport stone to build such monuments as Stonehenge, Avebury, Carnac and even Gobekli Tepe as the post glacial flooding after the ice age effected not only Europe but even as far away as Asia Minor thus allowing people to travel throughout these extended continents via inland waterways.[12]

---

12 https://www.amazon.co.uk/Robert-John-Langdon/e/B00DWSP368/ref=dp_byline_cont_ebooks_1

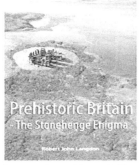

Prehistoric Britain
- The Stonehenge Enigma

Robert John Langdon

He even provides an evocative and (to some) provocative illustration of Stonehenge as being right on the edge of the sea, instead of being landlocked as it is today.

Almost all of his book are e-books, and although I don't like reading in this format I'll have to stop being so pure and buy all of them when I get back from holiday. I don't agree with much of what he says, but I enjoy the stimulus and the sense of 'What If?' that he inspires. Especially when he gets onto his detailed argument that Atlantis, as described by Plato, could only have been located in that shallow area of the North Sea known today as Doggerland! I know a lot of people with magickal sympathies who will fume and rage at that.

Incidentally, my dislike of e-books is because I used to be a Mobile Librarian, and saw the onset of e-books and Kindle as slowly destroying the need for such a service.

However, getting back to my burble, I think that we all have such Primordial Waters lapping at our everyday consciousness, and some refer to these as the Subconscious Mind that we must scry into if we are to get anywhere. Even so, I don't want to plunge into this type of Correspondence. That sort of thing has been done to death, by better writers than me. In *Keep It Simple, Stupid* terms, I'd like to imagine there's a lurking Power bubbling slightly in my own primordial depths and that I might emerge to become Atum-Re and sort out those muttering pharaohs.

Perhaps I'll be able to do this when we've been to the Isle of Wight and back – a place renowned by dowsers for its Dragon Energies.

As I prepared to settle down for the evening and watch something mindless on Netflix, I noticed that the bird feeders are all empty and there's not a sparrow in sight. I should fill them, and then maybe my own slight feeling of emptiness will go away.

An email just popped up from Trowbridge Library. They're talking about re-opening next week. *About time*, I say.

Then I got another email from my old friend Maxwell who is having lots of surprising synchronicities in connection with a couple of my books I'd sent him.

How d'ye explain this, he asks?

Magick dear boy, magick… is the best I can reply.

It's grey outside, not a hint of sun. Before I go and lock up, I must have a look at the frog pond and see if our microcosmic avatar of the Ogdoad is lurking in there, though I'll wager that he/she will only appear when Margaret is around....

Chapter 10

Apep was seen as a giant snake, or serpent, leading to such titles as *Serpent from the Nile* and *Evil Dragon*. Each night Apep encountered Re at a particular hour in the sun god's ritual journey through the underworld in his divine barque. The *neter* Set, who rode as guardian in the front of the barque, attacked him with a spear and slew him. But the next night Apep, who could not be permanently subdued, was there again to attack Re. The Egyptians believed that the king could help maintain the order of the world and assist Re by performing rituals against Apep.

M is in the Upper Room doing some on-line work with [N], hoping to understand something of her own inner wounds and torments from dark times in her past, and perhaps make sense of how, when she is meditating, she seems able to juggle energies between her hands like the figure in the two of pentacles.

I've been downstairs sprawling on the couch, doing that simple thing whereby I return to some semblance of Nothingness by reducing the letters of my name. Try it, it's surprisingly powerful. While breathing slowly and deeply, say your own name out loud and have a sense of the identity it expresses. Then say it again without the last letter. Then take off a letter at a time until you're left with the very first letter of your first name. And then utter...Nothing, and you can enter a place of your very own silent Namelessness. You can now feel yourself as being in the realm of **Nu**, also known as **Nun**, whose feminine and equal aspect is **Naunet** - *neters* of the primordial watery Abyss.

In a play of words the name is apparently paralleled with *nen*, meaning 'inactivity', as in 'I raised them up from out of the watery mass [nu] out of inactivity [*nen*]' This word, or state, has also been compared to the Coptic word *noun*, meaning abyss, or the deep.

I suppose what I'm saying is… lying on the couch apparently doing bugger-all, can also be a kind of Work

July 3rd 2020

This evening I did a final watering of our long and narrow garden before we go off to the Dragon Isle tomorrow for a week. I'll tell you later why it gets that name. At the far end of the garden, to the left of and just before the Faery Gate, is the Place where Time Stops. This was

another of M's brilliant ideas. We hang old stopped watches on the old and dying buddleia tree and try to create a small area of – no pun intended here – timelessness. Tucked into the corner, partially emerging from the Lady's Mantle, Mexican Fleabane, various unknown evergreens and random wild flowers dropped by random wild birds, is a small, ornamental 'Ruined Temple' that I got from the local charity shop.

You can imagine the sort if I can't get a photo: roofless, elegant columns, and the sense that it's been forgotten and left to rot beautifully in some ancient woodland.

It was there, for the first time in years, that I saw the frog.

Hello, Heket! I said. *Where have you been?*

I libated him with a very fine spray from my hose, but he didn't seem to like that at all and hopped into the nearby primordial and infinite depths of the little pond.

Well, I say 'him' but it could have been a 'her' – and perhaps in this tediously Woke Age I should perhaps use the term 'They'.

Sand Fairy Anne, as the Tommies would say in the First World War, deliberately corrupting the French *ça ne fait rien,* meaning 'It doesn't matter.'

I will take this as a good omen, but will make sure that as we approach the Isle of Wight on the ferry, travelling as if on the Solar

Barque, we will ask its permission to come here, and promise to be good.

Y'know, there's no rhyme or reason for the length of these chapters or the topics I cover. I suppose it's my Inner Sparrow dashing frantically at the food sources, attacking them at different angles, clinging on when necessary and sometimes finding myself upside-down. Often, the food falls away and the sparrows from our eaves plunge to follow it. I'm also doing this with my writing, I think, though not deliberately. An inner topic calls out *SKR*, and I have to take wing and go to it.

Before we set off on our holiday we topped up the Jachin and Boaz feeders, beyond which lies our garden. We put sunflower seeds in one and mealworms in the other. Within less than an hour the meal worms were gone and the sunflower seeds untouched. I guess our sparrows are carnivorous when given the chance.

I think this is all preparation for my next life as a sparrow on Lismore.

The hieroglyph above is for **Necropolis**. Apparently it also means **Butcher's Block**. I have corpses of reminiscence that I slap down onto a hard place and carve them into meaningful and digestible segments, that I don't need to sell you now. Thinking of the butcher's block reminds me again of the Bloodstone which had been used for exactly that: cutting off the heads of the Danes that Alfred's army had taken prisoner, knowing that the tide of the Danish dominance was turning at last. Despite the flurry of activities among myself and others a few weeks ago, the Mysteries of the Bloodstone have been silent. Perhaps it really has found peace. Not to mention, also, the long-ago souls in the nearby bowl-barrows that formed a small and local necropolis at a time and in an area where the population was miniscule.

As I scribble this on the eve of our holiday and the easing of the lock-down, I visualise myself in that small, lost valley and see it awash with the pure, bitter seas of the realm after the last Ice Age. In the earliest stellar worship in Khem it was believed that the waters of Nun would eventually inundate the whole world, and once again the universe would become the primordial waste of Nun's chaotic waters. Then I spent some time in my stillness visualising the Waters that once flowed over this entire area of Wiltshire, taking everything in my own world back out into the greater Ocean from which all once sprang.

I think that we all have such Primordial Waters lapping at our everyday consciousness, and some refer to these as the Subconscious Mind. At some point, in some way and at some level, instead of scrying into reflections, we have to submerge ourSelves in these.

So I haven't forgotten Sakkara. That particular Butcher's Block still exerts a certain presence – as a Temple of Death how can it not? We are all, of course, 'on our way out' every moment of every day, and succumbing to the cry of 'Come to me Quickly!' from those at the Other Side. If it wasn't for M I'd be happy to go now, and that's not a statement of misery or depression. I know where I want my ashes scattered, like Osiris, in 7 local places, after a no-fuss cremation. The Ancient Egyptian attitude to Death and the Afterlife, and their urge to achieve a mummified immortality in a necropolis like Sakkara is actually quite horrifying.

As it is, M insists that I live – healthily and strongly – for at least another 20 years, and I'm determined to achieve this for her sake.[13]

Finally, before we set off, I imagine that a part of me will *actually* be travelling to the mystic Isle of Khebit. This isle was guarded by the cobra, which was a symbol for the goddess, and you could only enter the sacred confines by assuming the form of a cobra, or scorpion. The rulers of the area, in pre dynastic times, called themselves 'He Who Belongs To The Bee'. According to some, the name Khebit means 'Swamp of the Bee King'. This is where Isis went to give birth to the wonderchild Horus.

You don't have to envy me going to a geographical location that some might rave about. You can create your own Mystic Isle within

---

13 She's just told me off, and insisted on 30 years.

your mind. After all the Isle of *Avalon,* has no tangible existence - Graham Phillips argued convincingly that the earliest descriptions of Avalon could not possibly have related to the town of Glastonbury. They were almost certainly descriptions of the isle we now know as Anglesey.[14]

Whenever you feel the need to give birth to some new, incredible idea or impulse, then you're already making your own holy, inner voyage to Khebit, or Avalon, or Hy Brasil or Shambala.

It is crass of me to say it, and clichéd, and possibly oh-so-boring of me to bang on, but these are all *within* you, wherever you are. And it might involve you with this little figure of the child king, that keeps popping up all over my messy manuscript:

More of this later...

---

14 See *The Lost Tomb of King Arthur*, Graham Phillips.

Chapter 11

Easily the most important divine vessel was the Barque of Ra which sailed across the sky each day as the sun. The solar barque the people saw during the day was called the *Mandjet,* and the one which navigated through the underworld was known as the *Meseket...* As the Barque of Ra descended into the west in the evening, it entered the underworld where Apophis waited to attack it. Apophis was present at the beginning of creation when, in one myth, Ra is the god who stands on the primordial mound and raises order out of chaos. Apophis wanted to return the universe to its original undifferentiated state and could do this if he destroyed the barge of the sun god and the sun god with it.

13ᵗʰ July 2020

We're back form the Isle of Wight now. I kept Khasekhemwy and Sekhemkhet at bay, although they tapped (or do I mean lapped?) gently at the edges of my thoughts like the tide outside our apartment. I don't yet know who or what they are, or what they might want, and especially I still don't know what they might offer me and - by extension – my readers. Perhaps the sea kept them at bay? It's an old folk-belief that witches or spirits cannot cross running water, and I always remember Dolores yarning to me how grateful she was to live on the island of Jersey, for the protection it provided in that respect.

For non-Brits among you, Wight is a large island off the southern coast. In the eyes of some it is situated at the muladhara chakra of the westward-looking Brittanic goddess and thus the source of kundalini energies. Some have dowsed colossal dragon powers in the geology and its fault lines. Gary Bitcliffe revealed that there is a rare geological layer of Upper Greensand that defines a serpent-shaped ridge, which runs through the centre of the island. Greensand is a hard crystalline iron bearing sandstone otherwise known as Firestone, because of its fiery colour. This might well be the cause of the many 'Fortean' anomalies experienced here. Others, equally drawn to the place, have seen the shape of the Isle as the outstretched wings of a dove, symbolising and manifesting the Holy Spirit. None of these, it seems, are contradictory. Wight has also been described as a druid fastness in ancient times, and even today it seethes with hauntings and time slips, and has numerous barrows and a few megaliths scattered across it varied landscapes.

The fact is, none of these drew us toward the Isle, and the hieroglyphs beginning this chapter simply mean 'Ferry'. We simply enjoy being near the sea with a vast array of walking trails across the landscape. I didn't want to keep a detailed Journal of the 'What We Did on Holiday' - sort, so here's a summary...

It took us some time to get up the hill from Mottistone to the neolithic Longstone, mainly coz I got out of puff, and was still

needing to build up my strength after the long illness I described in my last Journal. We had done this exact walk a couple of years before but I had no memory of this very imposing stone at all. I can only conclude that, on our previous visit, it had remained invisible. Not like in the Invisible Man stories though... I know from experience that sometimes places and stones like this don't want to be found. Presumably, we had wandered around the Mottistone Estate and been guided away from it.

I was pretty knackered (and I'll come back to that in a moment) but as there was no-one else there I circled it widdershins, talking to it, asking permission to be here, visualising myself as sinking into it. I can't pretend that I had any sense of cosmic/lithic/bonding revelations, but it felt like the right thing to do. I also noticed that in the fissures, a few people had placed coins. I put a gold pound coin in place, noting that the image of the Queen was prominent in all of them. So it was a sort of goddess offering.

Of course, someone was likely to come along and take the coin and spend it, but that's what it's all about. Many years ago Peter Larkworthy, a senior, influential and discreet figure in the Wiccan movement, told me about visiting the grave of Dion Fortune in company with Debbie Rice, who had been Magus of the Society of the Inner Light. He told me that some weirdo had placed coins on the grave in a particular pattern, with the gold coin at the centre, and silver coins orbiting.

Did you leave them? I asked.

No, we spent it at the pub, he chuckled.

I was delighted. It was me who had left the coins.

When Omm Sety [1904-8] wanted to say thank you to the goddess Isis for preserving the life of her friend Ahmed, she decided to do it in the Egyptian way. That is, it had to be a votive offering of the most precious thing she had. Her biographer commented:

> So she took off the necklace of blue amulets she always wore and gave it to my friend, asking her to place it in the niche of Isis in the great Hypostyle Hall of the temple, on the stone floor under the figure of the goddess. 'But', said my friend to Omm Sety, 'the temple is full of tourists: one of them will take it.' 'No matter,' she replied. 'Once made the offering may pass to anyone, as it used to do to the priests.' (who ate the offered food, et cetera.[15])

Because Omm Sety wanted her friend to have the necklace she had so often admired, she made the woman accompany her when she placed the offering at the feet of Isis, and then told her take it up and keep it for herself.

So I rather hope that the token offering I made at the Longstone might reach appropriate souls. Plus I know a lot of pagany types (including us) who leave offerings of various foods and liquids at various megaliths and barrows, and often for the faery folk. They believe that the 'essence' of these material substances is absorbed and appreciated, as is the actual 'effort' made by the supplicants. We

---

15 *The Search for Omm Sety,* Jonathan Cott

have often made the trek up to Tinhead long barrow and libated it with beer, and when I visited the large Headon Warren Barrow on the Isle of Wight last week, I did similar with just a fizzy drink as it was all I had. That site seemed completely dead to me.

Mind you, I mentioned the stone being invisible on a previous visit. During our whole week on the Isle of Wight I only saw two sparrows. I'm sure it's home to a million, but I can only say that 999,998 were invisible to me at the time and I did look. Our own house sparrows are having a massed riot outside this office. Their feeders are full. They still prefer the mealworms to the seeds.

14ᵗʰ July 2020

Apparently the comet Neowise has appeared in our skies. There's an impressive photo of it in the skies above Stonehenge, which is just down the road from us. I've tried to see it for myself, but no luck so far. The pundits say it won't return for 6500 years. Maybe that's what agitated Messrs K and K from their tombs in Sakkara and brought them into my head. Also, there's a satellite taking the closest ever pictures of the sun, so that should make Horus perk up.

We had lots of Little Adventures on our holiday last week that needn't be written up, but I did have two powerful khem-ish workings that I might outline now...

For the first time in years I had a bath. Don't get me wrong, I'm not a smelly old crusty worried about fluoride in our water. In our home we have a bath and two showers – one up and one down. I use the latter all the time because it's got the sort of power that can strip paint off doors – if I ever wanted to take one in with me. So I've never used our own bath, and on the Isle I rediscovered a small level of bliss. I also remembered I used to do an awful lot of magick just lying in baths in years gone by. When I lived in the enchanted cottage down Murhill I managed to summon, stir and call up a dragon from the barrow that I (and no-one else) called Bel's Tump, just along the valley. That's the thing about getting old. I'm not sure if I've told this story in a previous Journal, so maybe I'll come back to it.

However, on the Isle of Wight, which on another level was, for my purposes, the Mystic Isle of Khebit, I kept it simple. As I mentioned before, I did that thing with my Name, removing a letter at a time. On this occasion it took on more than usual intensity. Each time I removed a letter and said the new Name out loud I had a sense of, well, masks falling away. No, that's not *quite* what I mean, so I'll have to have a Good Think later... But what happened when I got to **Alan Richards** was that I had the briefest, teensiest glimpse and sense of a parallel life, but in this country and this time. **Alan Rich** was most certainly an American parallel life. When I got to **Al** (a name which I forbid anyone to call me) I necessarily resonated like a bell with all the Crowleyan connections.

These were all micro-revelations, and I haven't been able to repeat the experiences since. But I certainly got a good *Hmmmm* out of them.

Our apartment on Wight had large windows that stretched from floor to almost ceiling. We were close enough to the sea that when we looked out we saw nothing but the waves. We never watched the telly at all that week and would just sit and look outward, due westward, possibly slightly hypnotised by the changing tides, with our own memories floating up and down, getting swept away and then returning.

One evening, as the sun was setting almost directly before me, I decided to follow it, into the realm described by the *Amduat*, which was a funerary text of the New Kingdom. The Amduat, sometimes also known as the 'Book of What is in the Underworld', tells the story of Re, as he travels through the underworld, from the time when the sun sets in the west and rises again in the east. Each dead Pharaoh was believed to take this same journey, ultimately to become one with Re and live forever.

Understand that as you read the next bit I'm not detailing an astral projection into dread realms of the Egyptian underworld known as the *Duat* (sometimes spelled as *Tuat*). I'm describing a piece of internal game playing to see where it might lead, and show how it's relevant in the everyday world of everyone.

So as the sun went down I visualised myself on the Solar Barge, standing just behind Horus, and very glad that the mighty Set was at

91

the front, ready to take on all enemies and monsters that might be encountered. You can see him below spearing the dreadful demon of Apep. This image is taken from the 21st Dynasty *Book of the Dead*, and it amuses me that if Pharaohs Khasekhemwy and Sekhemkhet had seen this they probably wouldn't have recognised what was going on, any more than a Christian of the 1st Century would recognise much of the 21st Century version of that religion.

I had already prepared a summary of the stages of the Journey through the *Duat*, or *Tuat* and started by visualising the symbol for the latter, this being:

Despite the convenient term 'Underworld,' the *D/Tuat* was in fact given no specific location. Most often it was regarded as being under the Earth, but it was sometimes regarded as being beyond the vault of the stars - or else in those Waters that they imagined extended everywhere beneath the land. I once quoted from somewhere, without reference, that: 'It is the place of the formation of the living out of the dead and the past, the true meeting-place of time before and after.'

To me, rightly or wrongly, this symbol should perhaps be regarded more like a sphincter which is capable of being pushed, peeled, or pried open. Through that narrow entrance is the Underworld. It is the opened cervix leading to the womb. I also wrote a bit pompously and pretentiously in *Earth God Risen* that the Duat, or the *twat,* to use an English vulgarism, is the means by which we can give birth to ourselves.

You might think I'm pushing it a bit, but if you look at another representation of the Journey given below, see *exactly* where on the body of the goddess Nuit the boat is heading...

I figure that the linked symbol for the star, which so temptingly asks to be transformed into the pentagram, hints that the Stars and the Underworld are part of each other.

So I saw myself as entering through the symbol of the Tuat, pushing it open as I sat on the couch on the Isle of Wight, looking infinitely Westward. Of course I didn't do a 12- hour Working. No-one can or even should try to do this. Instead, before you start, it's instructive to find simple parallels between the Hours and your own life. For example, the moments when you've entered shadowy times; when you've felt you were drowning and no-one could see; when you've hoofed it down winding and twisting pathways, scared and anxious. So the summary from the *Amduat g*oes as follows, and I can almost hear Messrs K and K saying: *What's all that about, eh?*

- **Hour 1:** the sun god **Re** enters the western horizon, which is a transition between day and night.
- **Hours 2 and 3:** he passes through a watery world called 'Wernes' and the 'Waters of Osiris'.
- **Hour 4:** he reaches Imhet the difficult sandy realm of **Sokar**, where he encounters dark zig-zag pathways which he has to negotiate, to avoid being dragged onto a snake-boat.
- **Hour 5:** he discovers the tomb of **Osiris** which is an enclosure beneath which is hidden a lake of fire. The tomb is covered by a pyramid-like mound on top of which **Isis** and **Nephthys** have alighted in the form of two kites (birds of prey).
- **Hour 6:** the most important event in the underworld occurs. The *ba* (or soul) of Re unites with his own body, or alternatively with the *ba* of Osiris within the circle formed by the *mehen* serpent. This event is when the sun begins its regeneration; it is a moment of great significance, but also danger.
- **Hour 7:** the adversary **Apep** lies in wait and has to be subdued in chains by the magic of **Isis** and **Set,** and the strength of **Serket**.
- **Hour 8:** the sun god opens the doors of the tomb and **Horus** calls upon a monstrous serpent with the unquenchable fire to destroy the enemies of his father, Osiris, by burning their corpses and cooking their souls.
- **Hour 9:** they leave the sandy island of **Sokar** by rowing vigorously back into the waters.
- **Hour 10:** the regeneration process continues through immersion in the waters.
- **Hour 11:** the god's eyes (a symbol for his health and well being) are fully regenerated.
- **Hour 12:** he enters the eastern horizon ready to rise again as the new   day's sun.

(Bear with me while I put on another pointy-head version of a wizard's hat for a brief moment... These are not trips into the truly nightmarish 'Tunnels of Set' described by Kenneth Grant. I've scryed a bit into those too, but came away feeling dirty, as if I'd been wading in shit. Maybe others will rave about the importance of the Grantian 'Nightside', but I'm quite happy to avoid all that. Bill Gray opined that *Daath,* so beloved of Grant's Typhonians, functions as the Cosmic arsehole, and that all the stuff in its bowels and tubes should be left to decompose and then crapped out elsewhere in the Universe where there is a special place for it. As Osman Spare said: *Knowledge is the excrement of Experience.*)

If you're a passionate Khemophiliac (and oddly enough, I'm not), you could build a personal pathworking about all of these stages from the Amduat, but it's **Hour 7** that interested me most during this Wight Working...

Y'see there's a tendency to imagine the inner Beings or Energies of the Duat as utterly alien, and beyond our everyday experience. Of course there are dreadful Energies/Entities 'in there' and you'll need to have *some* insight into personal psychic protection. (But there have been towns that I've driven through both in Britain, France and the US when I've looked at the peoples around and prayed to the car: *Don't break down here, please don't break down here...)*

Look at Apep, known to the Greeks as Apophis, and who didn't seem to exist in the Dynasties of K and K. Its symbol was, you'll remember, as given on the right. There has been so much sensational writing about Apep that you might think it would need the Bell, Book and Candle-y sort of exorcisms to keep it at bay. But I'd suggest we *all* know Apep, and we've *all* encountered the twists and turns of this critter during our own Dark Nights.

Think of the times when you've going through life quite happily, on the surface, but suddenly find that old quirks and flaws of character from your past suddenly uncoil and wrap themselves around you, bringing paralysis or chaos. Someone recently, in his cups, bemoaned that he had damaged and ultimately driven away every woman who had ever given him love. Ironically, we were on a sort of barque at the time, and so he certainly knew Apep. For myself, a teetotaller, there have been many moments in the far past when patterns of circumstance surged up from the depths and brought me

95

Chaos and I whinged about the unfairness of it all, or babbled on about karma from previous lives – which I don't *necessarily* believe in, except when it suits me. Or you can find Apep in a bad neighbour, or in a troublesome car. Not that there's necessarily anything sentient in the latter, but Apep is glimpsed in the emotions of despair and torment that such a vehicle can create. At a time when I had two small children and almost no money coming in, my old, perverse and troublesome Peugeot 104 created such loathing in me that I would have thrown into the deepest Pit if I hadn't needed it so much.

You've all got parallel stories like this, if you scry back simply through your own experience.

So we need **Set** at the front of our Solar Barque, and I did a cracking essay about this *neter* in the appendices of *Dark Magery*, showing that there was a purity about this Being in the earliest of times. I argued that darkness is NOT synonymous with Evil, and that we need to find Setian qualities within ourselves if we are to defeat the Apeps in our own Night Voyages that are so often done in the cold and merciless daylight of Re.

And that was the essential drift of my Wight Working that night. It was not a hallucinogenic vision with pyrotechnics going off in my head and Fires of Hell licking at my mundane consciousness. Most of you will have got to this point in your own Work long ago, but it was another important *Hmmmm…* moment for me while M was fast asleep in the other room.

Chapter 12

According to the Egyptians themselves, their language was given them directly from the Spiritual World, by the *Neteru* or 'gods.' Certainly ancient Egyptian has similarities and common roots shared with some other ancient languages, though Egypt's claim that the very sounds comprising their language are themselves 'Powers' should not be dismissed lightly... But perhaps the best argument in favor of the use of 'reconstructed' Egyptian in these Rites is that Egyptian 'divinity' may very well still 'speak' the Egyptian tongue. [16]

\#

July 16th 2020

I'm still keeping Khasekhemwy and Sekhemket in their notional *serdabs*, scrying out through their narrow windows. Or maybe I should think of them as wrapped up in true mummiform fashion, unable to move or speak? Either way, I won't let them interfere with the pleasure of a near normal life. People are still being ultra-cautious, and many (not all) wear masks, and there's all sorts of measures in places regarding restaurants, pubs and public transport, and a few feel that 'Death will come on swift wings' to those who breach the social distancing guidelines, but...

Yesterday we were out in the woods with all our geeky walking gear, on a remote trail that might have been in deepest Wiltshire or deepest Gloucestershire – I'm not saying. In later historical times these woods were once once sacred to Appollo Cunomaglus, the Hound Lord, and also had a healing temple to Diana nearby, but these trees would have been sacred long before either of these. I've been in some fae places in my life but none to match this one. M whispered that it was like being in a cathedral, and I had to nod without wanting to utter a word. I've written in many places before about the quality

---

16 *HEBET EN BA: THE BOOK OF RITES.* www.spirit-alembic.com/egyptian.html

of Silence that is more than just absence of noise, but this was quite different. Every atom, every molecule, every fragment of soil and stone and tree and leaf and blade of grass was palpably Alive. We could barely speak for what we felt was true sanctity. Nothing happened. Nothing you could speak about. We just stood, humbled by the atmosphere, and both had a sense of what Gray would have called, with his passion for alliteration, *Perfect Peace Profound...*

Thank you we said, to the nameless, formless, Shining Nothingness that was utterly pure and holy.

It was on that same day on another walking trail that might have been in deepest Wiltshire or deepest Gloucestershire, we stumbled on this little house that had been built into a hollow tree trunk. It was beautifully made and I would say recently made, because there was a 'Visitors' Book' inside that only had a few signatures so far.

We were delighted, but I had to stop myself brooding upon the morons who would eventually come along and vandalise it. I quoted earlier that supposed curse from the entrance to Tutankhamun's tomb: 'Death shall come on swift wings to him that toucheth the tomb of a Pharaoh.' In fact there was no such curse on that tomb, but plenty on others that had been discovered over the generations. One of them was written up as:

Which means something like 'The Spirit of the deceased will wring the neck of any trespasser like a bird'.

I wanted to leave some sort of curse around the little house to protect it, but had to consider two things:

- It would just attract attention.
- My attempts at cursing in the past had always failed utterly.

Still, I had at least seen this wonderful little house at its unspoiled height, in the earliest days of its creation.

18ᵗʰ July 2020

A restless night last night. Went into the spare room. Not so much wrestling with Apep as being nipped by the Black Dog – the slight downers that come to me at unexpected moments, never lasting long, and never – I hope – snapping at those around me. During the night I woke at 3 am with the knowledge that I should call this book *Al-Khemy*, subtitled *Being in Two Worlds*, instead of simply *Khem – Living in Two Realms*, as it has been until now. *Al-Khemy* seems to me to work on three levels of meaning, and indulges my monstrous ego at the same time.

When I went in to bring M her morning coffee one of our sparrows edged along the gutter outside the window and got as close to me as any bird could, and began chirping. I think she was trying to tell me to cheer up or else that she wanted to have my babies

I've learned a lot about their noises lately. Single cheep notes between pairs is part of their courting or mating rituals. Females make a short chattering sound when chasing off other females, or when her mate approaches. A lone sparrow may begin chirping to attract other sparrows. I've also learned about another variant which has a disyllabic chirr-up, giving rise to an old English name for the house sparrow: the 'Phyllip sparrow' where the *phyll-ip* is onomatopoeic. It is the loudest house sparrow vocalisation.

I was pleased when I googled that. I've got a name – a *ren* – you can do all sorts of magick when the *ren* is involved. To me, Phyllip had just given me a 'voice offering', the hieroglyph for which is:

This is the sort of offering that Kings would give to their gods in the afterlife.

Does HRH Phyllip see me as a God?

Of course! We are *all* Gods and Goddesses.

I'll put out extra meal-worms for them tonight.

20ᵗʰ July 2020

At about the time that Khasekhemwy was organising large numbers of people to make his impressive funerary complex in the desert landscape Sakkara, small numbers of tribal people were making their own version amid the rolling green hills of Somerset. Stoney Littleton long barrow is a Neolithic chambered tomb with multiple burial chambers, located near the village of Wellow. I don't need to be secret about that. It's reached after a seemingly endless descent on a single track road that was only slightly wider than our small car, full of pot-holes, and with no passing-places. And then, after parking, crossing a faery bridge and a modest climb back up another hill to reach it. The last time we visited tiny lambs were leaping up and down vertically, filled with fun. I think they call it gambolling. I vowed then never to eat another lamb, and I never have. One day I'll become vegetarian – but not yet.

The barrow itself is, I learned years ago, aligned to the rising of Venus. Numerous seers have glimpsed a bull-headed shaman as a site guardian and I've always felt comfortable with this presence. There were other people there: a young couple who had cycled from Bristol, but were from Michigan originally; a young family passing by and going goodness knows where. We didn't do more than drink tea from our flask while sitting atop the barrow and thank the former occupants for allowing us to be here.

Khasekhemwy would have chiselled or painted inside his tomb something like the following:

which means *Giving praise to Osiris, kissing the ground to Wepwawet.*

At Stoney Littleton barrow there is simply an ammonite on the side  of the entrance; a survivor of the times when this area was once under the Ocean, and which must have seemed marvellous to whoever plucked it from the rich soil of Somerset. I think they must have thought it was like a star, because few of them in this area, at this time (c. 3500 BCE) would have seen the actual sea. The poor thing is half-broken now but you should still touch with your left hand and right brain and ask permission to enter.

It was while we were sitting and daydreaming that I half-remembered a lyrical phrase from the tomb of a woman called Senet, who was buried in the Theban necropolis, that I've only now tracked down here at home:

> I repeated favour before the king and advanced my heart
> further than my forefathers who existed before me.

Which in hieroglyphs was:

101

Of course I'm not fluent enough in hieroglyphs to reproduce the above off the top of my head. It was scanned from a variety of sources that you might want to use yourselves. But it seemed to strike a note for what went on in the small necropolii of Britain. On the barrow that day (and previous days at other barrows) it was a matter of respecting the labours that went into its building, accepting the spiritual impulse, and also the urge to make peace in this life and for the next, while feeling – or hoping - that you've progressed beyond all the things that your forefathers had striven toward.

Something like that.

And the simplest invocation at these places, made simply and with simple visualisation is: *The people who made this once knew Love – and so do I.*

Of course it's mawkish and cringe-making putting it in cold black and white text like that, but, but if you can summon up the *feeling* behind it, you might get a glimpse of the artisans and the common folk involved. And know that they appreciated you coming...

After, we went to Stowford Manor for scones with jam and cream. And it seemed in its small garden that the world had almost returned to normal. Stowford only opens in the summer months at best of times. In the late 1970s it had a certain notoriety as a kind of posh commune. Princess Margaret dallied there with Roddy Llewellyn, who was famous only for being famous and her quondam lover; plus the young aspiring actress Helen Mirren was known to spend the odd weekend there, along with other 'celebrities' of the time whose names are now dust. We sat in the garden and watched their sparrows under their ancient stone eaves, wondering how they managed to squeeze through the tiny cracks.

It struck me then why I shouldn't feel guilty banging on about the sparrows so much, when I'm writing about Khem...

Y'see, if you're new to the notions of Khem, the whole range of the various pantheons over 5,000 years is totally bewildering. The *neters* change their potencies and shapes and names. Their allegiances and connections in the 6ᵗʰ Dynasty, for instance, are subtly and sometimes totally different ten dynasties later. The *neters* and their 'stories' from Alexandria, Khebit, Aunu, Memphis, Hermopolis, Abydos and Thebes are impossible to put together into a simple, narrative like the cherry-picked stories from the Old and New Testaments that you might tell your kids.

I was only able to access the kaleidoscopic Mysteries of Khem because I stumbled upon Osiris, when in the early 1980s I visited the Spring of the Green Man, in Conkwell. Then, at first, I could only associate him with that sublime line by Dylan Thomas: *The force that through the green fuse drives the flower.* It could just as well have been the parallel British deity of Cernunnos, or Herne, or Cunomaglus. But Osiris seemed to stick with me, and the Library Angel did its magick, and piece by piece I managed to make some sense of the many and varied recensions.

Which brings me to the sparrows again.

When Phyllip (as I now think of Sparrow) first appeared I knew nothing whatsoever about the bird. Day by day, by observation, by curiosity, by looking up clues on-line or in simple books, I've begun to get some idea of that hidden world that is both before my eyes and hidden in my roof, above my head. As the other types of birds appeared – the magpies, blackbirds, jackdaws, crows, pigeons, robins and others – I was able to understand something about them too. Although jackdaws and sparrows, for example, are feeding from the same source and creating their own territories in various parts of their garden, by and large they have no contact with each other and no mutual support or recognition.

So I think the multiform, multitudinous Mysteries of Khem are much like those flocks. Even now, decades later, there are so many aspects of Khem and its *neters* that I don't begin to understand and don't even want to try (like the inner lives of the pigeons Lulu and El Chapo!). My advice to anyone wanting to access those Mysteries but don't know where or how to begin, is to choose one *neter* and one Mystery Centre and work outward from there.

Personally I'm rather fond of all that went on in Hermopolis, and because our *Inner Guide to Egypt* is now out of print, I'll include the whole of that chapter in an appendix to whet your curiosity. In fact you it might do so to such an extent that you'll find yourself diving into its frog-pond like Heket did in ours the other day..

21ˢᵗ July 2020

Sitting in the garden office at 6 am. Meatloaf the blackbird just looked at me with irritation as I made my way past him, and made no attempt to flutter away. H was after his worms and no great big gallumping human was going to get in his way.

M will be working on Skype in a little while and I will wander into an increasingly normal-looking town and get a hair cut. But I thought I'd mention, briefly, that quote at the very beginning of this chapter…

I'm not sure I'd entirely agree with what KHIRON, *aka* Kuei-Shen Hsien, *aka* Jerry Clifford Welch wrote there. I've always understood that the Inners communicate via telepathy or a communicative empathy in which sonics and phonics are irrelevant. I stumbled on his impressive website[17] ten years ago and tried to contact him but he had already gone to Amenti. His followers wrote of him:

> Born as Jerry Clifford Welch in 1948, the sixth of twelve children of a goat-herder from the desert of Arizona.. of Cherokee and Choctaw ancestry as well as Welsh and the ubiquitous Scots-Irish. Imagine a youngish Merlin who grew up among Red-skinned Cowboys; then give him the spirit of a wood-elf, a mind like the Library of Alexandria and the sense of humor of a five-year-old; then dress him up in the silk robes of a Tantric Buddha.. and you will begin to get a picture of his personal reality.

I don't get excited by people who describe themselves as Masters, although I suspect in this case it was a title foisted on him by his

---

17 http://spirit-alembic.com/egyptian.html

adoring pupils. However he gave some intriguing techniques that you can try yourselves, actually *voicing* the Egyptian for specific results.

> We live (according to the Egyptians) on no less than NINE other 'dimensions', including many which are so non-physical that we can only 'dream' them... yet they remain very important parts of our lives. This Rite can stimulate the awakening of the 'dreamer' within the Astral and Causal Planes or dimensions. Used before sleep at night, it can trigger vivid dream-life recall and the ability to direct your dreams consciously.

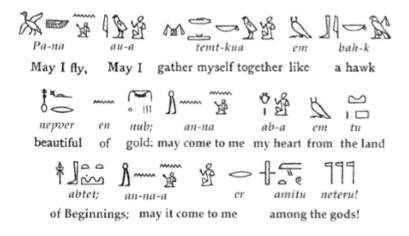

I can only suggest you try it yourself. Any effort in Magick is never wasted even if it might seem a bit silly, or way-out. In fact I'll have a go myself, tonight, before I go to sleep, and keep a print-out under my pillow. I'll let you know, as there are some problems I've always had with this notion of 'astral projection' that I haven't realised until recently. And later, when and if I think on, I'll have a long burble about ritual sonics and invocations and Words of Power and all sorts of things inspired in me by Phyllip's chirpings.

Meanwhile, I'm off into town...

Chapter 13

Hail, thou Disk, thou lord of rays, who risest on the horizon day by day! Shine thou with thy beams of light upon the face of Osiris Ani, who is true of voice; for he singeth hymns of praise unto thee at dawn, and he maketh thee to set at eventide with words of adoration, May the soul of Ani come forth with thee into heaven, may he go forth in the Matet boat, may he come into port in the Sektet boat, and may he cleave his path among the never-resting stars in the heavens.

from the Papyrus of Ani

July 22nd 2020

I had a go last night with that astral invocation given by Khiron. It actually felt rather good to say the words out loud when I got into the rhythm of them, and was able to match the sounds with sense. I went to sleep hoping for at least a glimpse of astral flight in the Field of Reeds, a jaunt along the Valley of Kings, or perhaps a dalliance with the Mu Dancers. Instead I dreamed that M and I had been given a week in Butlin's Holiday Camp in Yorkshire, with a room right next to the Bingo Hall. M was appalled and left, giving the whole camp a rating of 1 (out of 100) while I flounced after her but gave it a 6, coz I do enjoy a game of bingo. Then the rest of the dream involved someone trying to sell us a dodgy Camper Van for £10K. In short, an absolutely typical non-magickal dream of mine. I'll persist with the words though, on future nights, because they did feel good to gently chant.

The hieroglyphs at the top of this chapter mean 'Hail to you Ra in your rising, Atum in your setting.' While I find them quite charming and obviously enjoy cutting and pasting them into this manuscript, I don't think they have any intrinsic magickal power. Nor do I believe that Hebrew is a 'Sacred Language' and that those letters have the inherent ability to open doors to the Innerworlds and Intraworlds. Honestly, I'm not being jingoistic or a dreadful, narrow-visioned, small-hearted 'Little Englander' when I say that the Hebrew letters and the Egyptian hieroglyphs are no more evocative than the letters used in the national alphabets of your own country.

There's a wonderful and provocative book by French-Jewish researchers, the brothers Messod and Roger Sabbah who show quite clearly that the letters of the Hebrew 'alephbet', to give it the proper name, are devolved from hieroglyphic originals. That is, the Hebrew letters that so obsessed the magicians of the Golden Dawn and all their descendants, were not magickal keys given by YHWH, but derived from images that were once devised and carved by very human scribes in the courts of Khem.[18]

More of that later when I tell you about some extraordinary research done by my pal Judith Page involving sonics...

I had to confess to M yesterday that I hadn't been entirely honest with her when we were on the Isle of Wight/Khebit. I wasn't really struggling for *breath* as we went up hills in my post-pneumonial recovery phase: I was having a recurrence of the 'Old Man's' problems I described at gruesome length in *Dark Magery*.

I didn't want to get back to the doctor before our holiday because:

- the pains were by no means as extreme.
- he would probably prescribe more horse tablets.
- effects of said horse tablets and the attendant dietary regimes and other things would spoil our week away.

As it was I managed very well because, I think, I used a different kind of inner magick. I've tried many times in the past, for other ailments in other parts of my body, to speak to my cells and bones and muscles nicely, gently, calmly and respectfully. I don't think this ever worked. This time, on Wight, I got really angry and gave my aching bits and pieces strict orders to stop messing me about, commanded that they would stop the pain within five minutes and

18 *Secrets of the Exodus,* M & R Sabbah, Helios Press.

that they would NOT wake me at night or otherwise interfere with my life. And if they *still* wanted to mess about then they should do so with one of my other Selves – perhaps one of those pharaohs I've been writing about.

That must seem absurd but I've always been struck my Michael Talbot's hugely important book *The Holographic Universe*, in which he described how people with multi-personality disorders can be diabetic in one personality but totally clear when they're in another! So I figured that if I could nudge the aches across to another part of my intra-self, they would cease to trouble me, Alan, there on Wight and the Mystic Isle of Khebit.

I have to say that it worked, and still works now. It was only when M said she felt the energies of Wight felt very 'prickly' and subtly troubling that I suggested maybe it was *my* energies she was sensing and not the island's.

She gave me a Look and we had a long Talk.

I'll make an appointment in the next half hour to speak to my doctor...

24th July 2020

I've intoned Khiron's invocation for the past couple of nights but with no real success. My dreams are the same as they always are: mixtures of present concerns and old anxieties, all rolled together to create a narrative - a night-time 'yarn', often quite entertaining but too boring to recount.

I suppose what is nudging me at the moment is to get some clarity about the sonic aspects of Khem and my present-day magick, as triggered by listening to and learning from Sparrow the other day. I'll have to have a *yurble* now…

When I first learned about 'Words of Power' in my teens I was thrilled with the possibility. I'd have sold my soul to get those Words that might: open locked doors; give me gold; stop my Mam and Dad shouting at each other; and most of all get Lynn Maitland to take all her clothes off. Not necessarily in that order.

When I accessed what was available then from the Golden Dawn stuff the startling foreignness of those Words of Power (in Hebrew/Greek/Latin) gave them a splendour that had me vibrating.

How often did I call out those words from *The Sea Priestess*: 'Hear the invoking words, hear and appear: Shaddai el Chai and Ea, Binah Ge!' When I learned what they actually meant, that degree of potency faded, although there's no doubt that a good chant can still ripple the aethers as I hoped would happen with Khiron's stuff.

Later, when I saw the invocations in William G. Gray's *Seasonal Occult Rituals*, or in his privately-printed *Rite of Light* – or, yet further, in the various 'ancient' Wiccan rites that were being publicised then, I was dismayed.

I could write these, I thought, not with hubris, but with disappointment. They were crafted by human word-smiths of varying abilities, and were not explosive, electrifying sonic downloads from Higher Beings, even if Higher Beings *were* involved in the performance of the rites concerned - as I had (and have) no doubt that they were.

I suppose the best example of what I'm struggling to whine about, is the modern manifestation of my teenage imaginings: *Alexa* and *OK Google*: word/sound activated thingies that can connect you to... whatever you want.

You can scroll through ten thousand Invocations on the internet and see that they are all crafted by humans, using mundane words. If they work – and I've no doubt they do for the users – then it has to be because of the inner attitude and projective power of the user. Like the actors I talked about in *Dark Magery*, working from the inside out.

A teenage memory might explain it. In my secondary school (to Americans, a High School), we had a deputy-head teacher called Hazel Richardson – no relation. No-one ever messed with her. She could quell a riot by sheer presence. None of us could ever quite define what it was that she did, yet none of us would cross her. In contrast we had a delightful math's teacher whose name I will preserve out of respect and guilt, who said and threatened (very loudly) all the right things to try and quell the troublesome demons in his class (us), but without effect. I'm sure you've all got examples from your own schooldays.

Which means it's not the Words as such that are important, and so I doubt that the *words* quoted from the Papyrus of Ani had any effect whatsoever unless – somehow - they were connected with internal feelings.

Which brings me to vowels, and the extraordinary piece of artwork[19] done by my lovely pal Judith Page, entitled 'Vowel Sounds'. I've done a small black and white copy of it here, but you should go on-line and see the real thing in full colour. It was commissioned by John Stuart Reid, who was into cymatics to illustrate the use of pertinent sounds that would have been uttered by a priesthood over the granite sarcophagus situated in the Kings Chamber of the Great Pyramid of Khufu.

Cymatics, I had to google:

> Cymatics gives validity to the fact that everything that we perceive as hard objects, including our bodies, are actually continuously vibrating at their own rates..[20]

As Judith commented separately n her email:

> One has to appreciate the depth of meaning and practice carried out by the ancients, all of which is lost to the modern day person. The ancient Egyptians understood the meaning of a 'sick building' and employed the 'pi' - all researched and documented by R. A. Schwaller de Lubicz when he spent 25 years measuring the Luxor Temple - Le Temple de l'Homme.

As to the sarcophagus she depicted:

---

19 http://www.judith-page.com/album/PAINTINGS/EGYPTIAN%20PAINTINGS/slides/Vowel%20Sounds.html
20 https://ask.audio/articles/how-sound-affects-you-cymatics-an-emerging-science

'This sarcophagus is highly resonant, due to its high quartz content, hence the ancient Egyptian architect's choice of raw material as limestone and alabaster lack the resonant properties enjoyed by granite. John is of the opinion that vowel sound chanting in the acoustically enhanced King's Chamber was intended to have an energising impact on the sarcophagus during sacred rituals. A clue as to what such rituals may have involved is given by Professor I.E.S. Edwards in his book, *The Pyramids of Egypt:* *"According to one of the most popular myths the sun-god Re, entered the mouth of the sky goddess Nut every evening, passed through her body and was reborn at dawn. When he died, the King was assimilated to Re and was thought to undergo the same nightly process of gestation and rebirth as the sun god."*

'*Spell 430 addresses the god in the womb thus: 'You are restless, moving about in your mother's womb in her name of Nut.' It is particularly indicative that Djedefre, Khufu's immediate successor, should have chosen to have an oval, not rectangular, sarcophagus; it is really a representation of the human womb. As these texts show, the actual sarcophagus was regarded as identical with Nut and it possessed her maternal attributes.*

'If Khufu's sarcophagus symbolised the womb of Nut, it is reasonable to guess that it may have been used as part of their "rebirth" rituals prior to the pyramid being finally sealed. Noting that the sarcophagus resounds like a bell when struck, (although at a low frequency) John considered the possibility that the architect had engineered it to resonate at the pitch of sound (as distinct from the rate of beat) of a baby's heart since rebirth rituals were concerned with the gestation of a fœtus and the birth of new life.'

All of which is for me to say that you can make your own Words of Power by simple use of vowels, which you can regard as the 'soul' of the words – giving life to otherwise dead consonants.[21]

I think I've yurbled and ranted enough. I fear this might be getting boring. Am off to the doctor's surgery now to get my pneumonia jab. This jab promises to protect me from 23 kinds of pneumonia. I've had bouts of it twice now, and I don't want a third one carrying me off to Amenti just yet.

---

21 See Appendix 3

Chapter 14

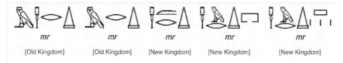

Some people call structures like the Egyptian Pyramids as 'Ancient Ruins', but we call them 'Perfect Bridges' where we can reach and touch the wonderful masters of the past! States have collapsed, empires have disappeared, epochs ended, new eras have begun, but the Egyptian Pyramids are still standing! Why? Because those who built these timeless pyramids had an endless desire to become part of eternity!"

Mehmet Murat ildan

25th July 2020

It makes you wonder about that sarcophagus, though. A sarcophagus is defined as: '...a box-like funeral receptacle for a corpse, most commonly carved in stone, and usually displayed above ground, though it may also be buried.' Is it just me, but how can you not want to lie in the one in the King's Chamber of the Great Pyramid? Outside the Tithe Barn in Bradford on Avon there is – or was – an open stone coffin that kids are always lying down inside until their parents snap at them, not wanting a *memento mori* at this stage. The sarcophagus in the pyramid is 198cm long, 68 cm wide, and 87cm deep. I couldn't fit into without curling up but I bet Napoleon could, and did, and I'd pay a King's Ransom to scry whatever it was that he experienced when he spent the night there alone. It's said that when he emerged the next morning, white and shaken, he refused to answer any questions about what had befallen him. Not until he lay on his death bed in St Helena did he consent to speak about it, only to halt almost immediately with the words: 'Oh, what's the use. You'd never believe me.'

Well, that's the yarn, although Napoleon's private secretary, De Bourrienne, who was with him in Egypt, reported that he never went into the pyramid and just did measurements outside. But what does de Bourrienne know, eh? He'd probably even deny that Napoleon had haemorrhoids. I'd rather have a stirring legend than the boring and paralysed facts. And by the way, remembering the naughty song that every boy of my age sang when we little (copying our war-hardened parents): *Hitler, has only got one ball/Goebbels has two but very small...* Documents have just been released that show Hitler really *did* only have one ball. I can't stop singing this now. To the tune of 'Colonel Bogey' if you don't know.

Just suddenly remembered something...

Years ago I did a series of simple workings in which I visualised myself as being in the sarcophagus of the Great Pyramid. What impressed me most was the overwhelming density of material weight beneath me. 'Weight' isn't the right word, so much as 'density', perhaps, as if the entirety of the Material World was pressing upward onto me. I had a sense of being propelled heavenward, as if the pyramidal top was the front of a spaceship and I was a pilot. I got frightened, and returned to the 'normal' world – which at that time was somewhere on Winsley Hill, with my second wife in bed next to me and my four little daughters asleep in the next room.

When the deeply psychic William G. Gray visited the Pyramids on the Giza plateau and also Sakkara, he had no such startling experiences as Napoleon might have experienced, except that he and the Sphinx had a moment of mutual recognition. What he did say in his autobiography is something that I've come to accept over recent years. I've probably imagined that I came to this conclusion myself, with my own inner Work and semi-scrying, but the fact is I probably just got it all from Bill, and forgot where it came from. He took issue with the Ancient Egyptian belief-systems, as regards the building of pyramids and the mummification of kings:

> So long as their bodies remained intact so would their personalities survive, but should these decay entirely then they might be reincarnated but without their former rank and importance. Naturally a king or noble could not face the thought of being reborn a slave or anyone of no social significance whatever, so every precaution was taken to

114

prevent this horrid happening. Apart from his body being preserved and carefully set into safety, his most precious possessions would be buried with him, and symbolic servants too, plus every artifice ambitious priests could think of in the way of special commemorative services and periodic prayers for his spiritual well-being in Heavenly happiness. They overlooked one all-important factor. The progress of evolution. Theirs would be a permanently ancient Egyptian heaven with no further developments or improvements to increase their experience. While other humans were advancing and expanding their spiritual growth through continuous lessons learned by living, those once wealthy and important people would remain staticly bound to out-of-date beliefs imprisoning their consciousness in comfortable cages of their own creation.[22]

So, am I in awe at the thought of Messrs K and K being in my psyche, somehow? No. Am I in awe at the thought of them being pharaohs? Not at all. They are the earliest version of 'Celebrities' – that glistening species which so infects and blights our present world. They crapped, just like you and I crap. And they probably had bollock pain just like I'm having (despite my attempts at Displacement Magick), for which I must visit my doctor, wearing a face mask, within the next hour...

Back from the doctors. Same old same old, but no horse tablets. I didn't tell him about the two pharaohs whom I've been trying to pass

my pain onto. (With increasing success I have to say. But I do use a particular archetype as an intermediary that I don't want to blab about yet – if at all.)

I spent the morning repainting the hallway while M was out walking on the hills with her pal Jo.

I hate painting, and am inept and famously messy, no matter how much care I take or how often I invoke Ptah the Artificer god before I

22 *The Old Sod* – Alan Richardson & Marcus Claridge, Skylight Press.

start – as I always do. I do think that *neter* (one of my favourites) does help out a bit. And whenever I use white paint I cannot *not* think of how the Pyramids used to look when they were first built: that is to say pure white with glass-smooth sides and a gold capstone. Mark Lehner did an excellent picture of this in his *Complete Pyramids* but – understandably - made sure the artwork was copyrighted. Even so, imagine how much the sun would explode off the white sides of the pyramids, making them seem as if they were on fire.

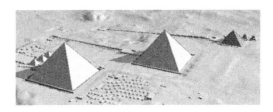

The basic story of how they were built uses the Step Pyramid of Djoser in the Sakkara complex as a kind of precursor. That is, the skills they used in building that (as designed by the mighty Imhotep), were later expanded upon and taken a step further on the Giza plateau. That makes perfect sense but – there's always a twist when you explore Khem – there is now evidence/speculation/suggestions that Djoser's pyramid actually came *later*.

That's quite an explosive thing to consider. It means that the Great Pyramid is actually much older than people believe, and that Djoser's pyramid was a magnificent but ultimately inferior copy.

Joe McMoneagle and his peers have always fascinated me, being professional scryers for their country. He is (I'm assuming he's still alive!) a retired U.S. Army Chief Warrant Officer, and was involved in 'remote viewing' operations and experiments conducted by U.S. Army Intelligence and the Stanford Research Institute. He was also among the first personnel recruited for the classified program now known as the Stargate

Joe is the first to admit that in remote viewing the sense of chronological dating is always somewhat elastic, but when he scryed the building of the Great Pyramid (and I'll come back to this soon)

he felt that the origins went back twice as long as historians and archaeologists had calculated.

To me, it doesn't matter if that's accurate or not. I gave up trying to make sense of Time aeons ago.

Does this take us into the fantastical realm whereby the pyramids on the Giza plateau were built using extra-terrestrial and/or Atlantean technologies that the present world has not yet rediscovered?

No.

Look, I've no deep interest in Atlantis, though I'm fascinated by any extra-terrestrial stuff – as much as I am by the Faery Realms. And that last statement is not a piss-take or a sneer.

In his *Ultimate Time Machine* McMoneagle scryed the builders using water and curious water-filled frameworks whose purpose was not immediately clear, though I might make sense of them in a moment.

Going back to Bill Gray, his senses told him that the blocks had been manoeuvred into position by men pulling ropes. Aware of the old tradition that Egyptian priests had uttered magic words that floated the blocks into place, he insisted that these were in fact 'work shanties' which the workmen sang with emphasis as they hauled on ropes or did anything with rhythmic effort. He also added stated that the stones, which had been cut from the Noquattan Heights across the Nile, had been floated over to the Pyramid site on huge flat rafts when the annual inundation took place. Although the water may only have been a couple of feet deep at the edges, that would still have been quite sufficient, he felt, to move the blocks.

Somewhere up in my loft I've got a book written by two engineers, in which they were quite certain that the Great Pyramid contained an *internal* ramp, of a curious square spiral shape. This meant that the slopes on which the smaller stones were dragged were no greater than 7° and therefore manageable. I didn't begin to understand the mechanics or the physics and knew that invoking Ptah the Artificer God would achieve nothing, but I remembered the broad details. They were mocked at the time, but only yesterday details have emerged, from the result of internal scans that were impossible a few years ago, that such an internal ramp does exist, in much the shape they had calculated through purely scientific reasoning. So Ptah was helping them, if any *neter* was!

But what about the monstrous huge blocks which formed the base of Khufu's pyramid? They fit together so precisely that you can't get a razor blade in the joins. How could they possibly do this with copper tools? Surely it was done by Atlantean lasers? There could be no reasonable explanation.

Actually...

In 2009 Professor Joseph Davidovits, the founder of geopolymer chemistry, wrote a book with the provocative title: *Why the Pharaohs Built the Pyramids with Fake Stone.* He had been intrigued by the absence of any chippings or broken blocks at any of the limestone quarries that provided the stone for Khufu's pyramid. Given the qualities of limestone and its tendency for splitting, there should have been a million tons of these lying around, even today. There were none. After stumbling upon some hieroglyphics mentioning 'liquid stone', alongside drawings of men who seemed to be tamping down the contents of wooden boxes, he asked himself whether the 'stones' were actually man-made blocks.

He then experimented and created a form of, I suppose you might call it 'concrete', by mixing dissolved limestone dust and rubble with natron, which was a form of soda ash found in abundance in Egypt, also used for embalming mummies. He felt that this would have been carried up the structure by packing into moulds made of thin wooden slats, well-oiled on the inside so as not to stick to the block during drying. And dry they did, very quickly under the hellish Egyptian sun.

Davidovits then made a few blocks of his own using this substance, the blocks themslves forming the walls of the moulds for the casting of other blocks. He marvelled that as they set, each would undergo tiny shrinkage to leave a 1 mm or 2mm line between its formative neighbours – for all the world like a finely crafted joint, made with anything but Atlantean or extra-terrestrial equipment. His blocks were indistinguishable from natural limestone.

In the same year his book came out, Michael Barsoum, a Professor of Materials Science at Drexel University decided to prove him wrong by using an electron microscope to scan the existing stones of the Great Pyramid. To his astonishment his scan revealed air bubbles and natural fibres within the structure of these monstrous blocks – two things that are never found within natural limestone.[23]

It's 9 pm and I'm knackered. My work in the hall this morning was somewhat disastrous. Instead of smooth white walls like those of Khufu's Pyramid, large chunks of plaster started to fall off. *Fuck fuck fuckity fuck* I hissed, so the nice people who live next door wouldn't hear me through the adjoining wall. And *Fuck fuck fuckity fuck* to Ptah the Artificer God also, whose input was non-existent, or else he hadn't a clue about artificing the walls of a late Victorian semi. I decided there and then that if M was cross with me when she got back I'd leave and never come back. As it was, she laughed. She'd had an excellent walk with Jo and had seen a herd of white harts - a highly mystical totem by any standards. She helped me clean the place up and soothed my fevered brow with an NCT in the Placebo – which is my schoolboy-ish way of saying a Nice Cuppa Tea in the Gazebo.

25ᵗʰ July 2020

Re-reading all that last, I think that pretty much explains to me **How** the Great Pyramid was built, although it doesn't diminish the utter brilliance of the architects and builders – who were free-born Egyptians and *not* Jewish slaves.

As to **Why,** well there must be millions of books out there seeking to explain that, and I've read large numbers of them. Was the Great Pyramid:

- a tomb?
- a chamber of initiation?
- a Power Station connected to the Earth Grid?
- a charging point for Extra-terrestrial vehicles?

The Pyramidiots, as they're unfairly called by the modern-day equivalent of De Bourrienne, create new ideas every generation. I'm more than happy with all of them. They are now as many and wild as the new lots of sparrows under our eaves.

---

23 See also *The Mysteries of History*, Graeme Donald

I know my next statement makes no sense, but I've sometimes thought that 'Ancient Egypt' is in the future.

As for the sparrows, we've noticed some of the latter have made house a little further along the guttering, closer to our bedroom window. They must have heard about the mealworms that the Big Nameless Ones leave out at regular intervals.

Apparently it's my last chance tonight to glimpse the Comet Neowise before it disappears for the next 6,500 years. A picture of it appeared in our local paper, the Wiltshire Times. It wouldn't reproduce here in normal colours so I've inverted them to give you an idea and enhanced the size of the comet.

It seems to be flying above the Bloodstone that occupied my mind so much earlier, although it's 64 million miles away and about as close as Khem is to me today.

Alas, I don't have binoculars to see it for myself, and to be honest I'd rather go to bed at 9 with a good book. M is absorbed in her Thrillers of the 'Murder Most Foul' sort while at the moment I'm re-re-re-reading Lawrence Sutin's superb *Do What Thou Wilt*, which should be compulsory for anyone interested in High Magick, even if the Magus of interest is as dreadful a human being as Aleister Crowley.

Who, incidentally, was a powerful energy behind the chapter in the Appendix on Hermopolis that Billie and I crafted. Or rather, Ankh-af-na-Khonsu was – but that's a weary yarn for another aeon.

Chapter 15

During the fabled First Time or Zep Tepi, when gods, or aliens, ruled on Earth, the waters of the abyss receded, the primordial darkness was banished, and the human biogenetic experiment emerged from the light...Within the void called Time and Space there are those who move from reality to reality creating the programs in which souls experience. They move through the place known as Zero Point, where matter and antimatter merge to create new realities. It is the place where positive and negative collide to destroy matter and recreate again...It is a place of awakening and a place of forgetfulness. It is the beginning and the end of all and everything. It is the home of the creational forces, those who bend and shape realities through sound, light and color.[24]

July ?? 2020

I've no idea what the date is, as I scribble this. The lock-down has added a layer of timelessness onto my post-retirement languor.

Even though I never saw Neowise in person, and had to scry its essence by proxy methods, I felt a bit sad at the passing of that Comet. I feel that, as we are all One, **everything** is connected: Neowise' appearance; Time and Space exploding from a singular dot in the great Nothingness; Atum's first ejaculation (with the help of Iusaaset the hand-goddess); the mini-Quest for the Bloodstone; the onset of the Plague with its masks; the proliferation of Sparrows in

---

24https://www.crystalinks.com/zeptepi.html

our eaves... All and Everything, in fact, if I might *homage* Gurdjieff's work for a moment. I might not be able to draw lines of light connecting these like umbilical cords, but I know they must exist.

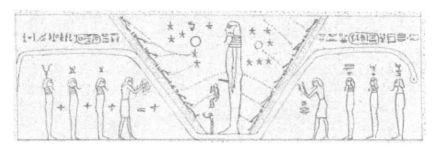

Sometimes I wondered if I made a mistake ripping my knowledge of the Kabbalah into a million pieces and scattering it across the landscapes of my mind. The QBL is the sort of philosophy that explains EVERYTHING, based upon the glyph known as the Tree of Life: 'The mighty all-embracing glyph of the Universe and the soul of Man' as the tag-line goes.

But to be honest, studying the Kabbalah was like reading the assembly instructions for IKEA flat-packs: no matter how abtuse, how bewildering, you have to start with the certitude that IKEA instructions are *always* right. It reminds me of that bit in *The Book of the Law* – or *Liber AL* – where Aiwass says: 'Change not as much as the style of a letter; for behold! thou, o prophet, shalt not behold all these mysteries hidden therein.' And – let's admit it – this sort of thing (QBL or IKEA) quickly becomes boring. Anyone who has ever

carried the multitude of parts for a 3 drawer, twin-mattress HEMNES up several flights of narrow stairs and then spent numberless hours and experienced Dark Nights of the Soul while assembling one single-handedly, will know what I mean. The invocation *fuck, fuck fuckity fuck* should be burned into the woodwork. Just never never **never** allow yourself to think that *They*'ve got the instructions wrong.

I had a deeply moving observation when I did my Brisk Walking across the Asda car-park this morning while M was in blissful attendance at the hairdresser for the first time since lock-down started. I saw a very elderly couple getting out the car, the husband with a shopping trolley and putting on his rather heavy-duty grey face mask, and the wife balancing herself on two walking sticks. He stood behind her and fastened on her matching mask, making sure it was a proper fit, then moved before her, made sure she was steady, whence they kissed, through the thick masks, and set off into the store.

I don't know who they were in mortal terms but on another level they were:

Osiris and Isis
Ptah and Sekhmet
Amon and Mut

Or if you like your Lovers viewed through a non-Khemical lens they were:

Mider and Étaín
Tristan and Iseult
du Lac and Guinevere[25]

I tell you what... I don't care how splendidly Khasekhemwy and Sekhemkhet exist in their non-evolving afterlives. Despite their harems and their armies, and their conquests and their servants and slaves and their incredible wealth (even by our modern standards), they will never know the truly alchemical gold of the kiss thatfiltered through the thick masks of that old and rickety couple in the Asda car-park.

---

25   du Lac told me he hated the name 'Lancelot', which was like a slave name.

M is in the upper room doing some on-line work with [N], involving a strong contact with an energy that shapes and presents as Merlin. We're both somewhat tired after a long walk on Roundway Hill, near Devizes, which in 1643 was the site of a major battle during the First English Civil War when a Royalist cavalry force won a crushing victory over the Parliamentarians.

To my shame, I know almost nothing about the Civil War – or even that there had been a *First* Civil War. I don't know many who do, although we can mutter about the Roundheads and Cavaliers without knowing much about what they stood for. Apparently more people were killed during this conflict than during the 'Great War' of 1914-18. Yet whatever antagonisms existed within the nation then, don't seem to have left too many scars on the surface of our mentalities today. Thinking of Civil Wars, when I lived in Kentucky in the early 1970s, I heard many people talk about how the South was 'gonna rise ag'in' but I don't know how intense or even serious they were in that respect. According to Melusine Draco in her *Atum-Re Revival* there had been some sort of civil war in Khem during the years of the 6th Dynasty. I'll look more into that, if I can, when I finally unleash the two pharaohs. Maybe this, too, is all part of what's going on. If there can be 'continuations' of characters, might there be 'continuations' of events? Perhaps there are Wars going in the Heavens, but fought digitally, in cyberspace?

God help us...

However, my interest on that height – a huge plateau – was in finding a long barrow about which I know nothing, and had only seen on the Ordnance Survey map. I can get quite obsessed about long barrows, as you might have gathered. There are as many speculations about their true purpose as you get about pyramids.

Long barrows were:

- Funerary structures for tribal entombment/interment.
- Places of initiation and transformation.
- Healing sanctuaries.
- Structures that produced Orgone energies.
- Centres for seership.
- Simple landscape markers.

I don't think that many have, as yet, associated them with extra-terrestrials.

I've also been re-inspired lately by Maria Wheatley's little-known  yet extremely valuable small book *The Elongated Skulls of Stonehenge*, that I actually think is universal in its importance. Elongated human skulls were once thought to be only found in South America. It has also come to light that they have been found in Europe, in places like Malta and Turkey, and of course you can find pictures of them aplenty with respect to the family of Akhnaton, that arch-criminal whom I must briefly write about later in this Journal.

Maria's thesis is partly summarised by the attitudes of early archaeologists who stated: 'Long barrows, long skulls; round barrows round skulls'. And here again, speculating as to why, there is the suggestion of Civil War even within the Neolithic and Megalithic cultures of Ancient Britain.

126

I had a *Hmmm...* moment when I read about the prevalence of long skulls in Malta though. We've often spoken about getting some winter sun, which is important to M but not to me, and the compromise we reached was that Malta might be perfect, with its background of High Weirdness and its Templar links.

Anyway, I'm getting distracted from my yarn about our Quest for the long barrow on the northern reaches of Roundway Hill...

Basically, as ever, I got us ever so slightly lost again. Dolores once told me that Anubis-types have an innate sense of direction, but that certainly counts me out from being an old dog-head. With the promise of heavy rain and me having left my waterproof in the car ('Trust me M, it won't rain, remember that I was once a Chinese Weather Magician.'[26]) - we were left with the choice of two routes to get to our destination. Despite the maps, it wasn't clear exactly where we were, and I vowed to write a stinging letter to the Ordnance Survey cartographers after this. So I did what I've often done in remote locations while in the near-Buddhic state of cluelessness: I asked for Help. Well, 'Help' is too strong a word. We were in no danger, none at all. But it was irritating, and I wondered if Powers were intervening and really didn't want us to reach the long barrow.

---

26 See *Dark Magery...*

Send us someone, was the signal I sent upward and ever inward, and this has worked in wild places across England and Wales over many years.

And lo, a single hiker appeared along the remote track almost waving the appropriate map at us.

Can you show us exactly where we are? And do you want me to wear a mask when I come near you?

Yes and No, she replied, cheerily, and I knew this was a manifestation of the goddess Seshat, the ancient Egyptian goddess of wisdom, knowledge, and writing, whose symbols are the leopard skin, tablet, star and stylus. She showed us exactly where we were and then proceeded on her merry way northward, through the distant golf course and toward the Imperishable Stars.

In brief, we never did get to the long barrow and the heavens opened and I got soaked, but happily so. Much later, looking on-line, it seems there's even some doubt as to whether it actually was a long barrow at all.

28ᵗʰ July 2020

Today I went to the barbers. The young lad did an adequate job but it wasn't as good as the one M had done a month before. Most of the time in the chair I was brooding about this notion of *Zep Tepi.*

In Khem, they had this thing about *Zep Tepi,* which means First Time, or even Golden Age, ruled by the *Shemsu Hor,* or Companions of Horus. There are any number sites on-line that give fairly precise dates for something that, for me, is nebulous. That's not say it's nonsense. I know Americans who look back upon the presidency of Reagan as an un-regarded Golden Age before the start of the Rust Belt and all the rest. I know Brits who yearn, similarly, for the years of Thatcher. And M was studying in Russia long before *glasnost,* when Communism was at its height; she marvels at Russians today who regard this as a *Zep Tepi* era for that Union.

But if we can remove all the human and political stuff I like to think of *Zep Tepi* as akin to those moments in the world when it was working as it should, when *Maat* ruled, who regulated the stars, seasons, and the actions of mortals and the deities, and who had brought order from chaos at the moment of creation.

I think it was R.J. (Bob) Stewart who coined the term 'Primal Land', which I think expresses what I'm struggling to describe here, although we might also think of it more clumsily as the Primal Essence of the Land. This was when the Land was pure, savage, beautiful and merciless – but actually **worked** in the *Maat*-ian way, before we came along and started to bugger it all up.

Even so, there are times when anyone can glimpse the luminous liminal line (God I sound like Bill Gray!) between the Yin and the Yang, and for brief moments see through the crack into how it was, and should be, and could be again – at least within ourselves. Is this the Faery Realm? I'm not sure. I had a *Zep Tepi* moment in that lost little valley of the Bloodstone. And we both did in those Fae woods I spoke about recently. But I think you can also glimpse it, or sense it, in those childhood memories of when things were – at least for brief moments - As They Should Be.

Bizarrely, one of the best writers for evoking this was P.J. Wodehouse [1881-1975], perhaps best known for his comic novels about the witless Bertie Wooster and his valet Jeeves. He had a prose style that was unique: poetic, comic and almost musical, and I admire him more than any other 'serious' writer. In the *Blandings Castle* stories, set in an English stately home, we follow the attempts of the placid Lord Emsworth as he tried to evade the chaos around him, which include successive pairs of young lovers, the machinations of his exuberant brother Galahad, the demands of his domineering sisters, and super-efficient secretaries, and anything detrimental to his prize sow, the Empress of Blandings.

It was Evelyn Waugh, a master word-smith himself, who summed up why Wodehouse left us all somewhat yearnful for a lost and subtle world.

> For Mr. Wodehouse there has been no fall of Man; no 'aboriginal calamity'. His characters have never tasted the forbidden fruit. They are still in Eden. The gardens of Blandings Castle are that original garden from which we are all exiled. The chef Anatole prepares the ambrosia for the immortals of high Olympus. Mr. Wodehouse's world can

never stale. He will continue to release future generations from captivity that may be more irksome than our own. He has made a world for us to live in and delight in.

Think back to your own past. Find a *Zep Tepi* moment, perhaps in your childhood, perhaps much later. I suppose you might think of this as a moment of *sartori*, but it's less overtly mystical than that. More a case of delicious melancholy or rose-tinted nostalgia.

I won't bang on more. You either get this idea or you don't. It's hammering down outside and I think I'll have a nap while M does her exercises in the upper room. When she's finished I'll go up and try to find that book by Maria Wheatley, as those 'Elongated Skulls' in the British countryside seem to whisper to me, and from some of them at least the word they whisper is *Khem...*

Chapter 16

The Egyptians were not fixated on the afterlife, as thought by early Christian translators but, focused on creating a higher type of human. This also links with bio-genetic engineering, cloning and alien experiments. Along with many ancient cultures, they believed DNA came from the stars and was destined to return and transform.

crystalinks.com

July 29th 2020

I stumbled on the hieroglyphs above in the *Hebet En Ba* website, which mean, according to Khiron:

> *I have made my way by the Tree of Life*
> *and I have brought myself to Silence*

I fancied that this said something about me, personally, but in fact for the past 47,000 words I've been anything *but* silent. So this brings me to a point where I must confess something...

I've been a little bit coy about how those two pharaohs chose to communicate with me via the Seer LM. Y'see, as I described at tedious length in *Dark Magery*, I had been suffering with the after-effects of pneumonia, but with overtones of what I coyly called Old Man's Troubles, connected with my 'tubes', as I would say – equally coyly – to anyone who asked. I wanted to find a healer, as all the orthodox medicines and antibiotics and pain killers were no longer working as they should.

I stumbled on the Seer LM, and she assured me that she could do hands-on healing. But how could I tell a young woman that the pain I was getting was all in my bollocks? She'd think I was an old perv trying to get a quick grope.

So I sort of hummed and hawed (at which I'm a Major Adept), ducked and dived (with the skills of Nijinsky), and eventually we agreed that she would a do an on-line reading to see if she could pick up any clues as to what might lie behind all this.

What she scryed straight away was a Cathar incarnation in which I had been hooded, tied dangling from a tree and burned to death, without ever revealing the whereabouts of my then wife and child. She felt that the fires then were what was causing the pain in my bollocks now.

I liked (and like) Seer LM very much and respect her talents, but this Cathar incarnation means nothing to me - although that doesn't mean it wasn't true. Over the years, with a geographical proximity to the late great Dr Arthur Guirdham, and all sorts of curious links between us, even though we never met, I've got used to having Cathars in my inner life, though never once have I felt a past life connection. This is one of these things that happens every now and again in this odd business of Magick… you get a fluttering of hidden things that burst out from the top of your head, like the avian guests in my eaves, then it all disappears. Very often you just have to let the fluttery things go, and make no attempt to trap them. Very often, it means bugger all until years later when these energies return in a different form, often bringing people with them. Very often it means bugger all, even unto the end of your life.

But it's all *Hmmm*-making, so you must go with the fluttering.

Am I stretching the sparrow analogies too much here?

Then… after her visions of my Cathar self – which weren't in connection with Montsegur – the two pharaohs arrived and demanded attention.

Even now, I still won't unleash them. They'll need a whole and separate chapter to describe what LM said and they'll get that in due course.

My first concerns now, sitting in the garden office during an apocalyptic rain storm, are:

What on Earth could they teach me?
What on Earth could I teach **them?**

132

I'm not being arrogant with the first question. Think about it… If I were to make contact, mentally, with someone 4,000 years in the future, what would I want? Of course, I'd have to ask the question: *What's it like?* Following on from that would be: *Did we all survive? Did we totally trash the Earth and its surrounding Space?* And in return, I'd wonder what I could possibly communicate to them that might be of use or interest. At the moment, I can't think of anything.

Now at this moment, 3.33 pm, I remember the Comet Neowise again and wonder what might the world be like when it returns in 6500 years time. I say *might* because I've a long list of prophecies made by seers who scryed into the future – none of which were accurate or even nearly so. I can still remember, word for word, the translation of one of Nostradamus' prophecies that I must have read in the 1960s: 'In 1999, between November 23rd and December 21st, the climactic War of Wars wil be unleashed.' I wondered, then, as a teenager, where I would be and what it might be like when this happened. As it was, in that very month, I was 333 miles away, on Winsley Hill in Wiltshire, and my much-younger wife and mother of my children was unleashing the apocalypse to get me out of the house so that her lover could come in and take my place. Nostradumus was pretty accurate as far as I was concerned.

However…

I mentioned the remote viewer Jo McMoneagle earlier, who scryed ahead and into the year 3000, and put his visions down for what they might be worth. He'd be the first to put his hand up to not foreseeing 9/11 and other events, but is always insistent that Time is a pretty tricksy wave to try and surf along. Even so, if he will be only partially right then I think it a world I might want to reincarnate in once my stint as a sparrow on Lismore is done.

He did note that the population then will be perhaps one sixth of what it is today. And listen to this:

> The population is very small. In searching for a cause, I sense that there were at least two great wars, but they were not the cause. There were terrible plagues that stripped the world – over six hundred years past – during a dark time

when men created germs that would not have otherwise seen the light of day. Now population controls are voluntary and precise.[27]

The crass old joke: *But apart from that, Mrs Lincoln, how did you enjoy the play?* - won't stay out of my mind; forgive me for including it now. Yet I would add that the rest of his visions are very appealing. The small, brand new cities he scryed as almost all being inland, away from the seas, and most were circular in design. They will be formed of concentric rings, with grassy garden-covered spokes running from the centre ring to the outer ring edges. The buildings are mostly glistening white with small-ish, stubby skyscapers. He even gives us a drawing:

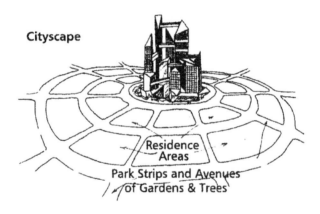

I know that among a few of my readers they will be thinking *Hmmm..this reminds me of someplace else, but involving water instead of earth* – and they're probably right. There are echoes there of the Plato's descriptions of Atlantis, of course. I'll try and come back to that in a moment.

Power in these cities will be provided by separate facilities that don't seem to have any moving parts. In fact, he scryed that unlimited power seemed to be a reality, and that in other places

---

27 The Ultimate Time Machine, p271. Joseph McMoneagle. Hampton Roads Publishing. 1998

across the globe they had power-generating machines that can alter space/time, although it is all kept local.

He scryed large sections of very old-growth trees where trees have never existed before. He saw manicured fields stretching as far as the eye can see, deliberately linked and folded together with large hedgerows of trees, parks and gardens diving the fields. 'It is a place where the diversity of plants far outweigh the needs of the masses, and the needs of Nature are being honoured instead of abused.'

Best of all, for me, he commented: 'I can see no evidence of the Old Testament.' Their churches, as best as he could define them, contained no statuary, no crosses, no candles, no low light, no religious imagery of any kind, and a completely different attitude towards what he calls the Grand Engineer.

Sounds a bit as though Ptah the Artificer Gid will be having a say upon the world, doesn't it?

That above is just a summary. McMoneagle goes into a *lot* of detail about many aspects of the Year 3000 and there is nothing wishy-washy or wistful about what he scryes. He describes a world that seems to me to be pretty damned good, as close to being Maat-ian as you might hope – though he doesn't use that term, of course. Once we get through the Wars, I think we will all be quite happy to be born into that realm.

And I think we must all doff our hats in this respect to Aleister Crowley. I can't remember now if it was his persona or that of Ankh-af-en-Khonsu who predicted that after the nasty, war-ridden Aeon of Horus we would have the Aeon of Maat, where things will balance with the light but infinitely powerful touch of a feather, and things will be true and just, and Nature and Man will be in adequate harmony.

It strikes me that Joe, if I can call him that, is having a glimpse of *Zep Tepi*, the First Time or Golden Era, but in our *future*, which sort of makes unsensible sense to me with my nagging feeling that 'Ancient Egypt' is in the Future.

135

Then again, if I can try to be a bit more precise, I really don't believe that Time is linear, although just for the convenience I have to speak as if it were. If anything, I reckon All and Everything is happening **At Once**, constantly exploding like Atum's ejaculation.

30ᵗʰ July 2020

In a few moments time it will be exactly 11.11 and I will tap the asterix key and have a whole minute of silence, visualising what I want for my – our – future.

*

There. I'm not sure if this current fad for 11.11 moments does anything, but it's worth a try. I think this is what Joseph McMoneagle was doing when he scryed into the year 3000: he was creating a template for what he thought could and should be. I would assert that when I used tarot cards years ago for that very same thing, it did always work, though never as quickly as I wanted.

I was busy in my garden office very early this morning and musing about the Ka statue of Djoser in his *serdab*, looking out at the Imperishable Stars. It struck me that I was in a kind of *serdab* here in the office, but looking out through the single window toward a row of Forsythia, Ribes Sanguinem (an ornamental current bush) and some swaying Escallonia. You can guess that I had to ask M for the names of these.

As I looked around the office I had a quick pang of mild shame. I had not actually cleaned the place since we had it assembled some 7 years ago. I'm notorious for being something of a Tidy Lad: healthy mind in healthy body and healthy (i.e. clean and neat) working area. I enjoy hoovering and mopping, and don't care who knows it. Over the years we've – **I've** - used this office to dump/store things that should really not be in there. And there are moments when I work in here that the screen of the computer takes on the role of a shew-stone and I get plugged into something, somehow. So this modest office is not so much a Magick Circle as a Magick Oblong, and I should be treating it with respect.

Right, I said out loud to the various spiders that lurked in a couple of corners. *In one hour's time I'll be back to hoover every corner of this place. If you're still here, then I'll take it that your Time Has*

136

Come and I'll assume the role of Osiris as Death God and not feel guilty.

So I did, and I didn't feel guilty, but I must say that if any spiders had remained they must have been very very small, coz I didn't see *any* as I wielded the nozzle of my ugly and ungainly Vax.

I did have one very awkward moment with the five-legged office chair that I had borrowed from a previous work-place (along with two industrial-sized bollards) over ten years ago. I was trying to get it through to door to make space for my tidying but it really seemed to swivel and twist and fight back.

Listen chair, I'm not throwing you out! You're not being dumped! Calm down...

And it did. You must think I'm a nut. But I really do believe that everything has consciousness of its own kind.

I had one of my long Celebrity Dreams last night. I won't waste your time describing it. As I've mused before, I don't for one moment believe that the Celebrity in question was making contact with me on astral levels – or any levels. I think in centuries past, before the Plague of Celebrity swept in, people would have dreamed of Kings or Earls or Knights or Queens or Ladies or Saints or Witches and Magicians.

I can say with confidence that this means my Higher Self (as far as I can visualise such a thing) is trying to bridge the gap to my Lower Self (me, my everyday consciousness) and bring something through. Or maybe it's the other way around?

We decided last night that on Saturday, August 1st, Lughnasad, we would go to The Cathedral – aka Avebury. It's one of my favourite places and just up the road from us. Several writers including Omm Sety and Joan Grant have opined that there were strong Egyptian connections with this place and also Stonehenge, that is just down the road from us, though I haven't been for decades. More and more these days we're learning that travel in those ancient of days was far more prevalent and reaching greater distances than was previously thought possible. Egyptians would have had no problems in visiting Britain.

But did their priesthood make their ways here to teach us a few things? Well, I think I'll have to devote a small chapter to this notion of 'Egypt in Britain' soon. It might be a conceit, but I'm sometimes inclined to think that the flow of teaching was actually in the other direction...

Chapter 17

The… astronomical priesthood of the British megalithic culture was actively involved in the design and layout of the pyramids. Whilst all the evidence shows that the people of Britain were far behind the Egyptians in terms of stone building and the production of bronze tools, they were clearly ahead in their astronomy and the adoption of complex multifunctional measuring systems. Critics might argue that any association between these two groups would have led to the adoption of metals in Britain at a far earlier date, but we have good reason to believe that this would have been anathema to the megalithic priesthood. [It] could be that…the Egyptian kings sent their builder-priests north to investigate the 'magic' of the stars understood by the people they had learned about.[28]

31ˢᵗ July 2020

I just learned this morning that the Egyptian New Year was on the 19th of July. Glad I missed it. I've always hated the phoney celebrations of New Year in this country, even when I was Up North where, traditionally, it is a big thing.

Got emails this morning from Rudolf Berger, a nice fella from Austria with an impressive magickal CV who did a podcast about me years ago, that I forgot all about; also Maria Wheatley, who told me that a revised and expanded and explosive follow-up to her *Elongated Skulls* booklet is in preparation. I also see that Nasa is launching another rocket to Mars, and that a documentary is about to be broadcast about what lies behind the Gantenbrink Door in the Great Pyramid. Apparently a new mini-robot has found never-before-seen red hieroglyphs, which they believe could possibly be gang marks made by the workers who actually built the pyramid.

---

28 *Before the Pyramids.* Christopher Knight & Alan Butler.

I'm sure all these things are connected in ways I will never fully understand. Meanwhile I'm off into town to find some paint remover to remedy the mess I made when rollered the walls last week.

August 1ˢᵗ 2020

A delightful day at Avebury. I'm sure that all of my readers will be aware of this place, and if you're not, then you might want to google it now.

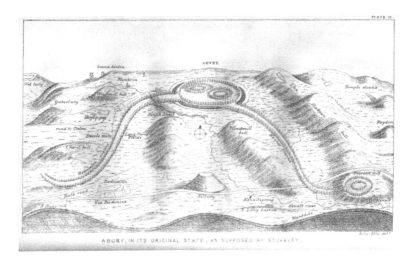

ABURY, IN ITS ORIGINAL STATE, AS SUPPOSED BY STUKELEY.

I've visited many times over many years and I suppose it's the pagan equivalent of Westminster Abbey or Canterbury Cathedral. I've been there before sunrise with my daughter Kirsty and we've seen – or rather felt – the huge white stones slowly dissolving out of the night and into the day. I've been there with M and watched a supermoon rise and fizz across the empty sky. I've been there in times of distress when I've had a long talk with a particular stone in the Avenue that I felt was 'mine' and poured my heart out. I suspect that anyone who has been along that Avenue with Khem-ist sympathies will know exactly what stone I mean. For me, even in broad daylight with crowds around, it almost comes alive to visible appearance and

140

shows its connection to trhe stars. If I had to give ita hieroglyph it would be:

But on most of the visits when I wasn't whinging I just had a banal nice cuppa tea and a Good Think.

The hieroglyphs at the top of this chapter mean – according to Khiron – 'I have entered into the Sacred Mysteries' and I do think Avebury has this effect.

This morning we arrived before the hordes and I was disappointed that there was not a latter-day druid in sight. Still, I was able to sing to the stones, one by one, using the Vowel Sounds I talked about the earlier, uttering the very souls of Words:

- Aaaah – while sensing Earth
- Eeeeh – (rhyming with *pair*) while feeling the Air
- Iiiii- - (rhyming with *see*) while feeling Fire from the Sun
- Ooooh – for the Waters beneath or moisture in the sky
- Uuuuh – more like a sibilant hiss, for the Mysteries of Spirit.

There is no 'right' or secret pronunciation. Work out your own. It's easy to give this 'song' a nicely rhythmic effect, and again what *you* do is correct.

I walked around most of the individual stones touching them gently with my left had and right brain, going deosil with some, widdershins with others.

M joined me with some of this, and at other times she did her own private thing and went very far inward. Some day I'll get her to publish own Inner Diaries. Although, the very moment I've typed this, I can hear her saying: *Not a chance, Big Boy!*

Afterwards, in the public area near the cafe, I had a nice chat to a splendidly garbed individual who self-described as a trans-shaman, here for a hand-fasting. (S)he insisted that I held the tall and quite impressive goat-headed wand.

In the bookshop I saw Maria Wheatley's little tome *The Elongated Skulls* squeezed almost invisibly between books that did not have one tenth of this one's value, so I pulled it out and put it on bold display.

And then we came home.

Did I have splendid eruptions from inner levels? No. Nor did I expect any. I long ago learned that – for me – the inner stuff doesn't work like that. But I knew that the *heka* – the magick – was very much there and will no doubt teach me things in due course.

The quote at the beginning of this chapter outlines the thesis of two men who are engineers rather than mysticks. I've got any number of similar books upstairs that expand on their ideas but from mystickal and magickal and even historical viewpoints. If I were to précis these now I'd quickly get bored. So what I'll do is tell a quick story...

The Brits, if I might call them that, went to Khem under the leadership of an individual I will call Abaris. Now Abaris the *Hyperborean* is an intriguing figure from a much later period who was adored and semi-deified by the Greeks, just as they did with Imhotep - whom they transmogrified into Asceplius. This proto-Abaris of mine is given the name – the *ren* – so I can get a grip of what might have happened.

Perhaps 'my' Abaris was one of the long-headed ones. I visualise him going to Khem and passing on his advanced knowledge of mathematics, measuring and astronomy to someone like the aforementioned Imhotep, who immediately applied what he learned to the building of Djoser's amazing step-pyramid at Sakkara, and even began one for Sekhemkhet, although that never was completed. The hieroglyph below means Imhotep, *He who comes in Peace.*

And so, after endless dynasties of relative stability, we get the arrival of Amonhotep IV as ruler of the Two Lands, who changed his name to Akhnaton and promptly did everything he could to suppress and destroy what we might think of as the Old Ways, in favour of his self-centred, person-centred, nasty, Celebrity Monotheism.

One of his daughters, Scota, married an outsider named Gaythelos, and they fled Egypt with a large following and settled in what we now know as Scotland.[29] After various confrontations they were then forced to leave and landed in Ireland, where they formed the Scotti, and their kings became the high kings of Ireland.

At some point during those persecutions a separate group of Egyptians, perhaps remembering the legends of 'Abaris', also fled toward the legendary Hyperborea, and, as outlined in Rendell Harris curious pamphlet from 1938, *Isis and Nephthys in Wiltshire and Elsewhere*[30]. This group landed in Dorset and made their way inland to settle near the village of Holt. Here, they resumed the worship of those two goddesses who had proved loathsome to Akhnaton. They now felt safer within the Green Land of Abaris than they had ever been in the Black Land of Akhnaton.

That, really, is as much as I need to say. If you're desperate to know more, even if only to destroy the thesis, then send out a signal and do some googling and you'll find all the information/false information you might need.

Personally, I'm not rooted into the historicity of The Story. After all, as I realised when researching *The Sea Priest,* there is not a shred of substance for Morgan le Fay, the sea-priestess from Atlantis. Yet I've known seers I respect who have undoubtedly drawn great magickal energies and teachings from the latter.

Listen, I honestly have no hard and certain beliefs about having had a past life in Khem. But there are undoubtedly certain brain-cells within me that get quite agitated by certain dynasties and their events. I suppose it's like tuning forks twanging together in harmony if just one starts.

You probably think I've been a bit harsh toward Akhnaton but I won't take back a word of it. He was *not* Moses. I could probably

---

29 See Lorraine Evans *Kingdom of the Ark*
30 Reproduced in full in *Searching for Sulis.*

write a whole book about that but my readers would die of boredom by the end.

Omm Sety despised him and compared him to the Ayatollah Khomeini. The scholar Donald Redford described him as a 'one-track minded, authoritarian iconoclast who impaled captives and deported populations'; a peer of his, Veronica Seton-Williams saw him as man who 'rode around in a chariot just worrying about his nutty religion'.[31] I'd put him up there with David Koresh, Jim Jones, Marshall Applewhite and Mike Ashley.

For some reason, people think that because he advocated monotheism that this was an evolutionary step forward. The same people have not a clue as to the true nature of Amun, or they wouldn't have made that assumption.

Enough said.

We're to Iford tonight where they're having open-air opera in what we think is a faery-haunted field next to the Britannia Bridge, where

we've had a couple of unusual incidents and I once felt the presence of Pan very strongly. We will sit on the grass at two metre intervals and hope that it doesn't rain. Actually, I realised recently that although the female figure carries a shield bearing the eight-fold arms of the Union Flag (very Ogdoad-ish that!), it's a straight copy of statues to Minerva across the Mediterranean world. I wonder if it's someone's secret *ka* statue? It might be ours! - we performed our own 'mystick marriage' at its base sometime in 2005, as I recall.

Before I move on to the next chapter – and I haven't a clue what it might be about – I must yurble about the pre-dream experience I had last night...

I couldn't drop off. My lifelong strategy for this is to give myself any one of a dozen lectures. In effect bore myself to sleep. One of them involved involves giving a long speech about the amazing but totally

---

31 Quoted in *The Search for Omm Sety* by Jonathan Cott.

useless rocket-powered aeroplane the Messerschmitt 163 Komet. Often, when the lecture ends, I simply daydream about getting into the cockpit and flying it around. There is no astral projection involved here. It's no more than a ladd-ish daydream like I used to have about playing football for England.

On this occasion I realised something with a jolt. Something which perhaps explained why I've found many path-workings or similar visualisations quite awkward or even impossible.

As I visualised the aeroplane aligned as in the picture above, I realised that when I climbed into the cockpit I could not turn 90° left. I had to turn the whole machine around to face the other direction and then I could slip behind the control quite naturally.

It struck me then – and I know this is absurd – that I had always been wrestling with the silver cord that (for many) connects the astral body to the physical. Dion Fortune wrote somewhere about getting a bit tangled with hers, and on the few spontaneous occasions when I've been (blissfully) truly out of my body, I've always been more fascinated by the nature of the silver cord than the surroundings.

Even though I was not astrally projecting myself into the cockpit of the Komet during this pre-dream day-dream, I was being thwarted by the subconscious *idea* of a cord, leaving my navel and trailing around the right side of my body. Which is why I could not, for example, visualise descending a spiral staircase anti-clockwise.

I tell this for what it's worth. It might explain something to others, too.

And while I think on, getting back to Iford and the opera, I know that if they sing *Nessun Dorma* I will cry. I always do. I can't understand or even, with my degree of weird hearing loss, make out the Italian words beyond the title (None shall Sleep), but the pure sounds, like the holy vowel sounds, wash right through. Perhaps as I tried to do for the stones at Avebury. Then when the sopranos kick in with untranslatable faery tones, I'm just undone.

Chapter 18

If ye are in Heaven or on Earth, in the South or in the North,
or in the West or in the East, my Moment is in your bodies...
a fragment of Khiron's *Invocation of Divine Identity*[32]

3rd August 2020

According to the news on-line for this area, it's hotter here than in Cairo. I'm in the garden office, looking northward, not to the Imperishable Stars but to M setting up two hanging baskets that will grow strawberries. We've just filled the feeders with mealworms and the sparrows are having ecstasies.

They sang *Nessun Dorma* at the opera and I was undone. Mind you the same happens in: *Love Actually* when Colin Firth goes to get his woman from the restaurant in Portugal; *The Parent Trap* when Lindsay Lohan says 'I *am* Annie'; *The Champ*, with Jon Voight and Ricky Schroder (that boy should have got an Oscar that year). There's scarcely a scene in that last when I'm *not* having what M calls a 'hanky moment'.

I had a fragmented sleep last night. Soon, perhaps in this chapter, I think I should let the two pharaohs out of their *serdab*. I suppose they've been lockdown too. Don't expect me to be writing about marvels, though. I mean, don't expect manifestations like Dorothy Eady's personal lover and pharaoh Sety Ist, who died approximately 3,200 years before she was born. Nor yet something like the great

---

32 http://spirit-alembic.com/egyptian.html

wolf-creature known as Fenris, that young Violet Firth accidentally summoned into her bedroom. I hope I haven't been bigging them up in the literary sense. I half suspect that it's not me they want to engage with, but someone reading this who will know *exactly* what's been going on below the surface.

I've got this theory that Magick, as long as it is done sincerely, **always** works, though rarely When you want, or How you want – but always when and how you **need**. Which can be damned exasperating. Stuff I did in my teens, usually involving Pan, took decades to make their results apparent. And the energies/entities/Beings that featured heavily in my previous Magickal Journals still float in and out of my life in unexpected though – for the moment - gentle ways.

Last yurble before I go get 'em...

I was pleased by an on-line article in *Nexus* this morning entitled: 'Robust evidence suggests human intention can alter physical systems.'

Someone had found a document within the CIA's electronic reading room outlining the finding that human intention can alter red blood cells. The CIA researcher expanded:

> We have conducted numerous bio-PK experiments in which both selected and unselected participants were able to alter significantly the activity of specific biological target systems, mentally and at a distance. In all of those studies, the amount of target system activity in the prescribed direction during a number of influence periods was compared statistically with its activity during an equal number of interspersed control periods. The obtained bio-PK results have been relatively robust.[33]

They're talking about my bollocks here, I think. And I have to say that my new technique for dealing with the pain by inwardly shouting at them does seem to be working. Y'see I trained as a teacher when I was a young man and learned very early on that if you tried to control a class by being friendly with them and treating

---

33 https://www.nexusnewsfeed.com/article/health-healing/robust-evidence-suggests-human-intention-can-alter-physical-systems/

them as equals then they will very quickly tear you apart - as that Maths teacher I mentioned much earlier found out to his cost. As *I* found out in my first year of teaching in Gloucester, at Saintbridge School. So although I still need to have more blood tests, etc., my strict technique, has been relieving the pain quite nicely.

But *sshhh…* don't tell either of them it's all a front.

Apparently, my calling them 'Pharaohs' is something of a misnomer. Specifically, the first recorded use of the title Pharaoh, using the hieroglyph below...

...is in the reign of the 18th Dynasty ruler, Thuthmosis III. So my two fellas from the 2nd and 3rd Dynasties would more properly be known as Kings:

often abbreviated rather sweetly to:

The family connection between 'my' Kings goes something like:

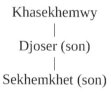

Khasekhemwy
|
Djoser (son)
|
Sekhemkhet (son)

But it's **Sekhemkhet** whom I have to talk about now because this was who the seer LM scryed first and whose story she recounted. In brief, as she attuned to me, a pharaoh came through forcefully. This was me, in a previous life, she said, although there was some dispute as to the legitimacy of his title.

He is with his brother, and showing him around a complex with pyramids.

Sakkara, I said, because I felt the place strongly if not the persona. I'm not sure the seer knew the name.

He is showing his brother the pyramid he is having built. It is still open at the top, open to the stars. He is very proud of it. And then he is attacked by his brother. He is murdered. His body was then hidden between great tilted slabs and completely concealed so that no-one will ever find it.

I said in an earlier chapter that during all this I kept hearing a rolling thunder of names: *Khasekhemwy, Khasekhemwy, Khasekhemwy,* 'although there was also an insert into the pauses that seemed to whisper a secondary Name, though not so forcefully – *Sekhemkhet.*'

The seer LM added: *There is also another pharaoh from another time. They were both you in previous lives.*

Well, do I see myself as having been a pharaoh – a King – in a previous life? In all honesty *No*, despite this flattering appeal to the huge ego I hide behind apparent modesty. Yet I don't doubt that LM was picking up two souls from Khem who seem to have business here in the 21st Century.

Without swamping my readers with details, here is the relevant stuff that I've found out about Sekhemkhet first…

Sekhem meant 'power' or 'might', and in recent years has been reinterpreted to mean the energy behind a system of healing. I suppose Reiki is the nearest equivalent.

Sekhemkhet Djoser-tety ruled in the 3rd dynasty during the Old Kingdom. His name was later Hellenized by Manetho to **Tyreis,** which I rather like, and I think he does too. That's a good *ren* to get a grasp of. His reign is thought to have been from about 2648 BC until 2640 BC. There's a relief of him showing the crowns of Lower and Upper Egypt respectively, that was found at Wadi Maghareh. Here, there were   extensive mines of copper and turquoise, and this suggests that these were exploited during Sekhemkhet's brief reign of less than 7 years.

On the Sakkara King List he seems to have been the direct successor of the mighty Djoser, as shown below.

As the seer LM had scryed, he did indeed start building a pyramid, and this one, sometimes known as the Buried Pyramid, was first excavated in 1952 by Egyptian archaeologist Zakaria Goneim. A sealed sarcophagus was discovered beneath the pyramid, but when opened was found to be empty. During excavations in 1963 in a different part of the complex, they found the mummy of a two-year-old child. 'The identity of this child remains a mystery. The only fact known for certain about it is that it cannot be king Sekhemkhet himself, since the king was always depicted as a young man.'

Given all this information it would be very easy to begin creating The Story, The Magickal Yarn that would 'explain' what the seer had scryed. Who was his jealous brother? Egyptologists have argued endlessly as to whether Sekhemkhet's successor was Sanakht or Khaba, but when I started to research them it was like falling down the rabbit hole, feeling that I would never get out. It was the voice of

151

my Higher Self whispering: *Keep It Simple, Stupid,* that rescued me. Though I must confess that I almost changed the injunction recently to *Keep It Simple and Short, Stupid* but M pointed out that people might misunderstand that particular acronym. Also, rather lazily perhaps, I'm hoping that 'out there' might be someone reading this who feels the message is for *them,* not me.

But what came to me again and again and again was that little two year old boy...

I would explain that I have a rather messy approach to my writing when I'm working on a manuscript. Using my pc, I mean. I work paragraph by paragraph, page by page, and when I find anything that might later be useful – ideas, images, quotes, hieroglyphs - I cut-and-paste and shove it all at the far end of the text. A lot of it I just end up deleting as the book progresses, and in the case of *Al-Khemy* I've removed: stuff about Olive Pixley and the time I was compelled to visit her brother's grave in Ypres; channelled stuff sent from insistent magi of various modern lodges; Atlantean insights; extra-terrestrials and hence my old pal Maxwell, plus a lot about my home town of Ashington and Newcastle United.

(Maxwell, I feel sure, is a definite modern-day 'continuation' of Abaris as far as I'm concerned, given his supreme knowledge of Maths, Science and other useful things that he would never let me copy at school.)

What I **almost** removed several times was this one tiny image of the 'child king' wearing the crown of Lower Egypt:

I don't know why I've felt this was important right from the start of the manuscript, and I can't remember where I stumbled on it in the first place.

Is this the Inner Child, the Wonderchild that lurks within us all? The still, small voice? Is it connected with the little mite who had been concealed in Sekhemkhet's pyramid as a peace-offering perhaps, or simply as a murder victim?

If anyone has any ideas, I'd love to hear them.

An afternoon of pure hell. I'd come back from town in a state of excitement; all the cafes and eateries were serving food and drinks at half-price as part of the Chancellor's drive to get us spending again after the worst of the lockdown. I'd rather hoped to take M straight back out for a bacon sarnie at Boswells.

Have you got pharaohs in your head? she asked me gently.

Actually, my little lotus-flower, they're Kings, not Pharaohs. But no, at the moment my head is All Quiet on the Amenti Front.

Well then, could you finish painting the stairs and the landing?

I might be a helluva holy mage but I'd just fallen for the oldest trick in the Book of Coming Forth by Day.

So I manned up and did all I could not to inflict chaos on our staircase walls and landing, and I pretty much succeeded. This time I *didn't* invoke Ptah the Artificer God before I started, although it took me the better part of a Yuga[34] to finish. By which time all the cafes were closed.

M was really pleased.

Did you take down the pictures and mirrors before you did the walls?

Am I not a Master Craftsman? I asked, and suddenly found a great need to go and replenish the feeders for the birds.

(I was in such a bad mood that I left said pictures and mirrors *in situ* and simply rollered and brushed around them. No-one will ever notice, apart form the odd bits of paint on their frames. I won't let her see *this* confession when she looks for typos in my on-going manuscript.)

August 5ᵗʰ 2020

I have to release the very noisy Khasekhemwy now, who was the sixth and last ruler of Egypt in the 2nd Dynasty c. 2775-c.2650 BCE. Oddly enough, when I first told M about him she had already heard that name when doing some Work with [S] some years ago. Not being able to put shape to the name, and not having much interest in

---

34   A cycle of 24,000 years

Khem, she assumed from the sound that it was Native American and thought no more of it.

There is not much known about this king other than that he led several important military campaigns. He re-united Upper and Lower Egypt after a civil war between the followers of the *neters* Horus and Set. Some believe he defeated the reigning king Seth-Peribsen, after returning to Egypt from putting down a revolt in Nubia. According to the on-line *Encyclopedia Britannica:*

> Khasekhemwy, whose name means 'the two powers have appeared', is the only king of Egypt to have selected a royal name that commemorates both Horus, the god traditionally associated with the living king, and Seth, his trickster brother; the emblematic animals of both deities are depicted above his *serekh* (the stylized rectangular frame in which a king's Horus name was displayed).

154

For me, his history is less important than that *serekh*. One of the most significant *neters* in my own life (when I'm in my *khem-ical* phase that is) is the one of Horus and Set combined:

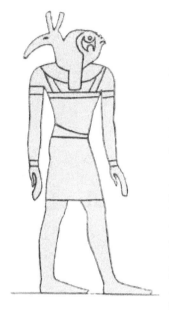

I wrote a lot about this being in Dark Magery so I don't want to retrace my steps here. You either 'get it' immediately or you're perhaps turned off by the inelegance of the glyph.

I emailed Normandi Ellis about the names Khasekhemwy and Sekhemkhet and she replied:

Khet is I think flame or fire. It's sometimes connected with incense. There are lively images of a brazier with a Sekhmet headed snake outside the healing room at Edfu. It contains various prescriptions for healing/visions art balls and incenses. **Kha** has a number of meanings depending upon the determinant of that accompanies the word. So it could be a flowering plant or it could mean to carve or it could mean to cry, or it could mean a column or a pillar of something. It's also a number 1000. So that doesn't entirely answer your question but maybe it can be helpful.

Before I press on with my Kings, I must have a quick yurble here, or rather quote directly from my own book *Earth God Risen,* that the lovely Skylight Press did a few years ago:

When I was a young man of 22 I spent some time in the University of Kentucky. I didn't go to America to study, I went to find my soul-mate and thus the True Love and Happiness I felt sure was over there. Someone who would, for once, be able to share this 'other' side that had always dominated and sometimes bent me out of shape during an era when such things were hardly known. I took a class on Creative Writing with Wendell Berry. I'd never heard of him and didn't know he already had a fine reputation as a writer, as well as being something of an eco-warrior decades before they coined the term.

One of the girls in the class – the only one I fancied – was lithe and leggy, with an exceedingly pretty face, long hair, a quiet presence and lovely voice. I was dreadfully shy in those days but made a clumsy attempt to chat her up. I got nowhere. I don't think she even realised what I was trying to do. I saw her around the campus often, always with a wistful sense of regret. My only consolation was that she would never have understood my 'other' side.

You will have guessed the punch-line. I was staggered when, several decades later, I realised that this girl who couldn't possibly have understood my 'other' side had translated the *Egyptian Book of the Dead* into modern, sensuous, evocative prose, as *Awakening Osiris*, and is now one of the authorities on Khem, and with a doctorate to boot!

August 6th 2020

It's 5 am. Working in the office. Even the sparrows aren't up yet.

I rather hope to finish this by August 8th, even if I have to leave loose ends. I didn't know, but apparently this is when a cosmic alignment called 'The Lion Gateway' takes place. It is held to be a time of increased cosmic energy flowing between the physical and spiritual realms. This gateway is marked by an alignment between the Earth and the star Sirius. As the star Sirius rises in the sky, Orion's Belt directly aligns with the Pyramid of Giza, and from our perspective on Earth, it appears that Sirius (the brightest star we can see) comes closer to the Earth. This is the point where the Earth is in alignment with the Galactic Center of the Universe. This allows the powerful portal to be in play for an energetic acceleration for our awakening.

As you can guess, I googled all of the above and make no judgement on any of it.

Far more importantly, this is when our four girls and their four fellas and their seven children will meet us at Pythouse Kitchen Garden near Tisbury, on the border between Wiltshire and Dorset. Because of the lockdown this will be the first chance they've had to celebrate M's 60th, which happened last month when we were on the Isle of Wight. This is, trust me, the finest place of its kind in the galaxy whether Sirius is shining down on it or not.

As I've sat there in the past amid the sublime gardens, I've looked south toward the rolling hills of Dorset and had a sense of the refugees from Akhnaton's miseries making their slow but safe way toward me and I couldn't tell you whether they had long skulls or not.

I don't know what they've bought M for her birthday. I rather hope it's something we can both use. Such as a new Dyson hand-held vacuum that can replace the stupid Saturn V-sized Vax I lumbered us with.

I feel that I'm coming to an end of my yarning with respect to my Two Kings. I don't suppose I'll find a quick answer as to what they want, what they are, and what relevance they might have to my own world. I certainly don't take fire with the idea, as expressed by the seer LM, that they were previous incarnations. If I were to arrive at a K.I.S.S. conclusion it might go something like this...

Messrs K and K are clearly aspects of mySelf. I don't mean that in terms of past lives, although that may well be the case. But... if **All is One** as I deeply and truly believe, then they are also parts of *your*Self too. Alas, I don't have the sort of psychism that can relay coherent 'messages' to my everyday consciousness. That is, I will never hear one of these odd and lost Kings saying to me: *Alan, now get a grip, because what has been happening is....blah blah blahdy blah...* I can only bumble through their energies and make sense of them in differing ways by looking for modern parallels, or *peshers*, as they might say in a totally different context.

It strikes me now that one of the biggest fears they had in Khem was that their name – their *ren* – would be forgotten. Maybe this is all they have wanted during this Journal. After all, before you read this, had you ever heard of Sekhemkhet and Khasekhemwy? Or knew anything about that little mite in the pyramid? Perhaps you might give the latter a name of your own choosing, light a candle for him one night, and dream about what he might have become. We'll do that tonight. You should too. Most of us have got a Lost Child within us, sealed in *serdabs* of our own making.

I still daydream about Sakkara at odd moments. Do the actual spirits of such places come to obsess me? Yes, I suppose they do. Or at least not spirits of the Hammer Horror Film kind, but something more in the way of echoes, or 'tones' to use that word again. There's nothing too mystical about this. You've all experienced similar. Think back to some piece of art that really struck you, the atmosphere of which lingered on, even though the actual image itself was no longer in front of you. Think of some movie you have seen that had the same effect long after you got home. Or, more likely, remember a piece of sublime musick that once burrowed into your soul. The images of Djoser's step pyramid and the drawings of the underground complex have a similar effect upon me. I don't know why.

It's odd, or not, and is perhaps an age thing (which I regard as a positive effect) but I could spend ages in chronological time looking through the king lists of Sakkara. That's not weird. I also go on the *Ashington Remembered* website, and muse upon the old photographs of the classes and schools I attended in my youth, i.e. from birth until

18, thinking *Who are these people around me?* It's the same with the *neters* - but that's enough of them for now.

Yet here, now, sitting in my garden office as the sun creeps up, in my heart of hearts or *ab* of *abs*, I am an Ancient Brit and I don't feel any dichotomy therein.

But I do sometimes think about those Two Kings in the impossibly distant 2nd and 3rd Dynasties and imagine them in their Timeless, perfect, unchangeable realms looking out at the Imperishable Stars and wondering:

Why do I keep getting sore bollocks?

Appendices, and other Mutterings

I like Appendices. I'm sure that, like myself, if you're really enjoying a book you'll break off at intervals to see how many more pages you've got before it ends. In contrast, if you *haven't* enjoyed the book then the appendices offer it a chance to redeem itself – though it rarely does.

I hope you enjoy the ones that follow...

Appendix 1

Photo sent to me by the late Maria B, of the SRIA

Look at the room within the glass. Look at the 'faery' in the shadow. I'm indulging in Pareidolia, I know, but...

Appendix 2

excerpted from

Short Circuits – Essays in Otherness

22 Shades of Gray

The next most important book to be written about the Western Magical Tradition for the 21st Century should be about the Hermetic Order of the Golden Dawn and its extraordinary system. I would suggest that the title and the theme be simply *They Got a Few Things Wrong.*

The problem has been that we're all in thrall to the intellectual genius of McGregor Mathers and in awe of the visionary talents of his wife Moina. We tend to see them as rarefied beings, austere exemplars of the Magical Arts who are closer to the Gods than us mortals. We tend to project onto them a kind of papal infallibility and rarely have the nerve to challenge what they created.

If we could 'remote view' the Mathers when they were creating their system we would see young Moina, fresh from art college and doing nothing worthwhile with her talent that her parents would approve of, seemingly in the shadow of the jobless and apparently unemployable man who wanted everyone to call him McGregor. Don't see them as grey-haired ancients: see one very absorbed and very young woman working at the behest of her slightly older uber-intense partner. Admire their passion and excitement as you watch them bringing through their teachings by means of the intense psychism we expect of them, augmented by techniques as surprising and unreliable as the dowsing pendulum to give them a straight Yes or No from the Mighty Ones, and also – surprisingly – the Ouija Board. Admire, but don't be in awe. They were, comparatively, mere youngsters when they did all this.

They did their work – or rather their Work – in grotty rooms, with never enough to eat, never enough light in the evenings, and no clear certainty that they would ever get any material profit from their efforts. They were almost like a couple today from the Benefit Culture except theirs came, eventually, not from the state but from the largesse of Annie Horniman, who was one of their first neophytes and most loyal supporter.

I'm not being denigratory here. Mathers was *the* great magus of the past 150 years. No-one else has come close. And as far I personally am concerned, I fell in love with Moina when I first saw that photograph of her at the Slade College of Art and nothing has changed since.

But they were very human, and very fallible when it came to putting together their system. Some of the rituals, like the Lesser Banishing Ritual of the Pentagram, are like steam engines which generate enormous power and proceed with a kind of majestic but clunking beauty throwing out sparks, steam, and a lot of wasted energy.

I think it was the kabbalist James Sturzaker who argued that Moina got 75% of the Colour Scales on the Tree of Life wrong, but because she got them right at Briah-tic levels, they still worked.

In a number of cases their apparently inspired system of Correspondences just do not correspond. They get results, as we all know and have experienced, but sometimes it's a case of fitting square pegs into round holes. Which actually can be done, and quite easily, if you've got a big enough hammer and bash the pegs until the corners splinter.

And in some ways they were cursed by the felicity of the number 22.

The 22 paths on the Tree of Life, 22 letters in the Hebrew alephbet (this is not a spelling error), and 22 cards in the Major Arcana of the tarot were crying out for a neat and obvious fit.

The initial match was done simply by putting the first tarot card on the first path and matching it with the first Hebrew letter - which was also a number. (I have to confess that I don't even know what letter/number this is, because I've deliberately never learned Hebrew, and reject the notion that it is a 'sacred language' when the letters are demonstrably simplified version of much older Egyptian hieroglyphs.)

A few magicians such as Crowley, Frater Achad and Paul Foster Case determined their own systems of tarot/Tree correspondences, but they never ventured far from the original, and were all still hooked onto the Hebrew letters.

It was an outwardly tough but inwardly warm Englishwoman called Bobbie Gray who, in the mid-60s, said to her husband: "Why does it have to be in bloody Hebrew? What's that got to do with us here?" Her husband Bill, too old to be an *enfant terrible* but most definitely something of an *eminence grise* by this time, looked at the whole Golden Dawn system and agreed. Working at remarkable speed and with serendipity of funding, he wrote a little known book which turned Mathers' system on its head.

William G. Gray's *Magical Ritual Methods* is a work of pure genius. Just one chapter alone, on ritual sonics, is still light years ahead of anything that is being done today. His version of the Banishing Ritual, for example, is superbly elegant and wonderfully simple, using a ring-pass-not kind of structure which utilises the concepts of Time Space and Event, and four (English) vowel-sounds. The whole book has been plundered, stolen from and used without acknowledgement so often that today, two generations later, there is a whole breed of young magicians, witches, kabbalists, Rosicrucians and druids who imagine that their techniques derive from the ancient temples of Greece, Rome and Egypt – or else from the dark, primordial glades of the Wildwood. But they don't: they came from 14 Bennington Street in Cheltenham.

Gray didn't take sole credit for his sublime system of tarot correspondences. He told me quite candidly that these came directly from his inner contact with the spirit of Dion Fortune. Likewise, when he detailed these correspondences in the large and later tome *The Talking Tree*, Bobbie told me that when she was taking down his dictation she often couldn't tell whether it was Bill speaking to her or Dion. I make no judgement on this, I simply pass on what was said.

Bill (or was it the spirit of DF?) showed that the Waite/Rider Tarot had an inherent system of cohesion that didn't need anyone to bash their square pegs into round holes as they developed their magic. He ignored the numbering of the cards and instead went for their sense, matching the positive cards with the right-hand pillar, the negative cards with the left, and putting the Moon/Sun/Star on the Middle Pillar. He described the right-hand pillar as being concerned with what he termed 'anabolic' or building-up energies, while the left-hand pillar expressed the 'katabolic' or breaking-down processes. And the cards reflected this.

Much of this is encapsulated in the following table:

Left Hand Pillar	Middle Pillar	Right Hand Pillar
Hermit		Hierophant
Death	Star	Emperor
Hanged Man		Temperance
Devil		Empress
Blasted Tower	Sun	Strength
Chariot		Lovers
Magus		High Priestess
Fool	Moon	World

They are conjoined by Judgement, Justice and the Wheel of Fortune, which Gray defined as Fatal or Karmic on three distinct levels of compensatory energy.

But there is also a cohesive integrity between the cards from top to bottom, as well as right and left: The Fool and World might be thought of as un-initiated, inexperienced humanity: the know-all, and the person who is wrapped up in himself. Above them are the High Priestess and the Magician, balancing each other in the appropriate way. While at the very top of the Tree are the Hierophant and the Hermit, teaching humanity by precept and example respectively.

Look at the Hermit from the Waite pack: if his staff represents the Middle Pillar, the lamp is at the place of Binah. What is the Magical Image of Kether? - an ancient bearded king seen in profile. What are the colours of Binah? Why is he standing on a mountain-top? Really – and just forget those damned Hebrew letters for once - where else could the Hermit go but on the path between Binah and Kether?

Connecting Binah with Tiphereth is the Hanged Man. His head is radiant (in the Sun), his legs are crossed to form the astrological symbol for Saturn, which is the 'mundane chakra' as they used to say, for Binah.

And then there is The Empress, connecting Chesed whose Magical Image involves regality and a throne, with Netzach, whose  Magical Image invokes a beautiful naked woman. There is even a heart-shaped shield next to her throne which bears the glyph of Venus, the planet of Netzach. All right, The Empress isn't naked, but look at the beautiful naked female figure of The World which connects Netzach with Malkuth.

Every card in the Waite pack, using this system of correspondences as determined by William Gray and inspired by Dion Fortune, comes alive when put in these contexts. Those readers who were in a sense 'brought up' by the Golden Dawn system and wedged tightly into it, might find the whole thing disturbing. But look through, and give it a go, and be prepared to be astonished.

However, if the title of the next book on Mathers' system should be *They Got a Few Things Wrong*, it should also have the subtitle *But They Did Their Best.* And they did it magnificently.

Which is no more or less than we all must do in this business of magic, no matter how primitive our early efforts might seem.

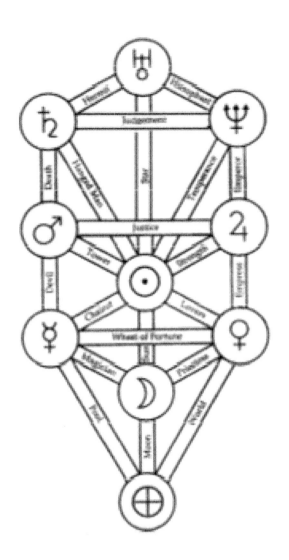

Appendix 3

Egyptian Alphabet

Sign	Trans.	Equiv.	Sign	Trans.	Equiv.	Sign	Trans.	Equiv.
🦅	ꜣ	a	🦅 or ⌐	m	m	▭	š	sh
⸝	i	i	⌇⌇ or ⸫	n	n	⊿	ḳ	q
⸝⸝ or \\\\	y	y	⬭	r	r	⌣	k	k
⌐⌙	ꜥ	e	🏠	h	h	⬯	g	g
🦅 or ℓ	w	w,u,o	🎗	ḥ	h	⌓	t	t
⌙	b	b	⊜	ḫ	kh	⊐	ṯ	tj
▫	p	p	⊶	ẖ	kh	⸚	d	d
⸜	f	f	⸗⊶ or ⎮	s	s	⸡	ḏ	dj

Vowel Invocations by William G. Gray

EAST	SOUTH	WEST	NORTH
INHALE	HOLD	EXHALE	EXCLUDE
OOOOAY	EEEOOO	HOOOAH	HAYEEEE
SUNRISE	NOON	SUNSET	MIDNIGHT
AIR	FIRE	WATER	EARTH

In the decades after he first created the above, he modified those apparently absurd sonics given in the third line and used the vowels: **Eeh, Ii, Oh, Aah** *– with* **Uu** *as the central 'sound' for Spirit. There is no correct way to voice/intone these. Try them out yourself until you find what feels right.*

Mithraic stuff that I found

EAST	SOUTH	WEST	NORTH
MMM	ĒY ĒIA EĒ	ŌŌŌ AAA EEE	YĒ YŌĒ

Appendix 4

HERMOPOLIS

In the whole of Egypt, no centre was more bewildering than Hermopolis. On magical levels, no place harder to get to. Its modern name is El-Ashmunein, but in the ancient world it bore the name - curious even to Egyptian ears - of Khemnu, meaning the City of Eight.

The actual site of Khemnu, today, contains less in the way of remains than almost any other centre in Egypt, excepting the solitary column at Heliopolis. Although it stands in a broad and fertile area of the River Nile's valley, only the merest fragments of temples survive above the general rubble.

Up until 1820 there were still two rows of columns from the hypostyle hall of Thoth's temple, although these dated back only as far as Alexander. To the South of these was found an earlier pylon of Rameses II, in the foundations of which were hundreds of blocks from the dismantled temples of that dismal entity Akhenaten; while elsewhere there is the entrance to a temple of Amenemhet II, and a fragment from a temple of Amun dating back to the 19th Dynasty and Seti II . . . but not much more.

Rubble and mud is the basis of Khemnu today.

A few miles to the West, near Tuna el-Gebel, is the site of Khemnu's necropolis, and also the catacombs dating back to the Persian king Darius I, which were actually devoted to burials of the sacred ibis and baboon . . . but little more than that.

On any level you approach it, the spirit of Khemnu is very hard to find.

*

We can enter Khemnu with the hare, which is seen on
on the standard of this the 15th Nome of what is
now Upper Egypt, or the South, that area itself coming
under the aegis of the Vulture as opposed to the Serpent.

It is with the hare itself that we can actually gain a clue: that strange creature of madness and leaping and great procreative powers and - as far western folklore goes - of witches and spells and tides of luck, and dances beneath the moon.

We can actually ride into Khemnu on the hare's back if we want, though if we are to see any more than shadows then we have to adopt something of the hare's vision and look at the place with eyes that are more animal than human.

*

Eight deities were worshipped in Khemnu and we have their names at least: Nu and Nunet, Amun and Amunet, Heh and Hehut, Ke and Kekut. Four pairings of male and female.

That at least is a start. Once a Traveller has access to a name, a *ren*, then he can begin to look for introductions.

According to the devotees of the Hermopolitan Recension, these were possibly the oldest gods and goddesses in Egypt, although by now we will have heard that refrain in almost every place visited. Yet in the case of Khemnu there may be some justification in this claim. All of the main centres can feel old, but none of them quite match the overwhelming sense of antiquity projected by this shadowy City of Eight, as the name translates. According to some, the original mound from which Egypt sprung was supposed to have appeared here. Sometimes, when you stand amid the phantoms and hear the wild cries of the sacred birds and beasts, and feel the hair rising on the back of your neck as a direct response to the surge of adrenaline, it is possible to believe it without question.

The deities were grouped into four pairs which carried the titles Night, Obscurity, Secret and Eternity, and bore the heads of frogs and serpents, although cats sometimes appeared also. The goddess Nunet, for example, was sometimes shown with the head of a cobra surmounted by a disk, and sometimes with the head of a cat. Sometimes Heh is serpent-headed, other times he is pure frog. Looking into the hierarchies of Khemnu is like staring too intensely into the darkness outside our homes: eye muscles weaken; fixed objects seem to shift; the familiar and expected can transform themselves into anything.

171

We can give a notional and debatable tabulation as follows, bearing in mind that in truth the deities of Khemnu writhe together like vipers mating in a nest, and it is always difficult to see where one ends and another begins:

Nu/Nunet	Amun/Amunet	Heh/Hehet	Ke/Keket
Abyss	Hidden Ones	Obscurity	Darkness
Eternity	Secret	Inertness	Nothing
Infinity	Invisibility	Mist	Night
Matter	Energy	Time	Space

The list can be endless, but it cries out for at least one interpretation: Out of the Abyss, in the Mists of Night, the Hidden Ones emerged.

While on another level far down the scale of manifestation, on animal levels of symbology, we could say that from their hollows in the mists of night, the hares emerge...

Khemnu is an atmosphere rather than a doctrine. A place where wisdom is attained through inversions, much as Alice found when she stepped through the looking glass. Other recensions were based upon an androgyne deity emerging with a cosmic burst of light and consciousness to take his place upon the land, but Khemnu emphasised the opposite of these qualities. In the crude sense, the priests of Khemnu knew that without darkness we could not appreciate light; without nothingness we could never have somethingness; without not-knowing we could never have true gnosis.

The Shu Texts of the First Intermediate Period (which were known to be heavily influenced by Khemnu) preserved the phrases: 'in the infinity, the nothingness, the nowhere and the dark', and also, 'where the Universal Lord dwelt when he was in the infinity, the nothingness and the listlessness', and again: 'when the Waters spoke to Infinity, Nothingness, Nowhere and Darkness'.

All of which once more allude to the concept of Nun, or Absolute Nothingness, developing a 'centre' from which manifestation proceeded.

It was from the writhing, cosmic mating dance of the Ogdoad that a primeval egg was formed from which a bird of light burst forth saying: 'I am the Soul, the creation of the Primeval Waters... my nest was unseen, my egg unbroken.' This was the Great Cackler—perhaps the origin of the esoteric notion that the Universe began with a raucous shout of laughter.

There are strong elements of Khemnu in that concept which holds that man has no soul (in the modern sense of the word), only a potential. This potential is comprised of dark and primitive aspects. Only by working on these can a true spark be developed. Only through inner work and suffering, and the confrontation with the darkness, can we begin to shine.

Even that is not exactly right. But amid the shadow-temples of Khemnu it is as near as the Eight will allow for the moment.

*

After the hare it is the ibis which can take us a little further into the city.

To the Egyptians, the ibis was a perfect symbol for their nation because its white plumage showed the sun, its black neck the shadow of the moon, its body a heart, its legs a triangle, and it always appeared at the rising of the Nile. The ibis relates to Thoth in the same way that the falcon relates to Merlin.

The name Thoth is a corruption of Djehuti, or Tahuti, whom the Greeks identified with Hermes - hence Hermopolis. In this area of Egypt he was seen as a Moon God, intimately connected with tides, and madness and matings, and wisdom of a reflective sort, whose sacred animals were the ibis itself, of course, and also the baboon, which in some households was kept as a pet, trained to pick fruit and even help with simple domestic chores. As one who rescued the Eye of Horus after it was stolen by Set, Thoth is in Khemnu to ensure that the shadow-aspects of this centre do not lose touch with the light entirely.

Thoth appears in many guises throughout the vast array of Egyptian mythology, and although he was respected and admired he never quite attained the public appeal of the likes of, say, Sekhmet and Hathor. Many of the gods began their theological careers as

173

philosophical concepts which, sometimes, attached themselves to human figures from myth or history. Christ was seen in Jesus, Geb in Osiris, but this process never developed with Thoth. He was always the Teacher, Assessor, Communicator, Interpreter, Balancer and Reflector of (Moon) Wisdom.

In any case Egyptian symbology appealed to the masses through the ages in differing ways at differing times. We can best understand this in the modern microcosm of the cinema and the concept of Hero. At its simplest, Hero was enormously handsome, wore a white hat and lived by black and white rules. As the decades (and perhaps the decadence) progressed, Hero became more complex, and sometimes even ugly. He became Anti-Hero or Reluctant Hero, and functioned in a variety of realms beyond that of mere adventure: sexual, intellectual, political, romantic or moral... each role backed up by the appropriate visual and musical symbolism.

The Ancient Egyptian would have understood Hollywood only too well. The Ancient Egyptians actually invented the dream factories.

And so the role of Thoth in Khemnu, surrounded by these strange deities from the primordial mud and slime, is not quite the same as the Thoth from other centres. This one is more concerned with that basic law of Nature which states: Learn - and learn fast. He is concerned with man rising from the animal and herd-responses without in any way rejecting or scorning the potency of these. Thoth knows how we are put together; who better than him to teach us about the *ka*, the *ba*, and the *khaibit*. It is the latter, indeed, which is his own special concern in Khemnu. It is the latter which we can adequately translate as - the Shadow.

*

Although Kha'm-uast would have identified eight aspects to the occult constitution of each individual, in the strange world of Khemnu we need only concentrate upon three:

The *ka* was the basis of everything. It was linked with what we would now term the personality, but it involved more than that. Like the personality, which seems to be given to us at birth like a rolled-up scroll containing our possibilities, the *ka* has determining factors

174

built into it. Like the muscles of the arm, the *ka* (and the personality) can be developed. Just as the arms are the means by which we control and manipulate the material world, and the personality the way that we relate to society, so is the *ka* the means by which we can progress.

Placed vertically, the arms of the *ka* reach toward something beyond the mundane world, toward the gods themselves. Placed horizontally, as the breast-muscle structure in the glyph indicates, the *ka* is the means by which we embrace and relate to other living beings - human or animal. In many cruder texts the *ka* is linked with male generative power and (indirectly) with epithets such as the 'Bull of Truth', and 'Victorious Bull'. Today we might echo this when we ask someone if they have the balls to do something particularly risky; in Khem, they ask the same person if they have a strong *ka*.

Of course not everyone has much in the way of a personality, or *ka*. In these cases they often compensate by filling the void with the fundamentalist aspects of religion instead, or submerge themselves within herd or mob mentality. Not much in the way of balls among this lot. Not much in the way of *ka*. But it is the way that we can all go with a weak *ka* and a strong *khaibit*.

The *ka* itself is dependent upon the Heart and the Name. The symbol of the Heart is another glyph of dual associations.

First, it is an obvious pitcher which can respond to the usual imagery such as 'my heart is filled with...'; and second it can be seen as a simple representation of the actual organ, with the apparent handles being truncated valves and arteries.

The *ab* was regarded as the centre of Intelligence. The *ab* sent impulses throughout the body via the blood. The intelligence

175

concerned is that particular spark which enables us to survive in this world by sheer awareness.

The symbol of the *ren*, or Name, is a mouth above water,

This recalls those obscure kabbalistic traditions in which initiates would only utter the Divine Name with their lips only just above actual water, in an echo of God speaking upon the Face of the Waters. The *ren* is our ability to define the world, to bring into focus those perceptions discerned by the *ab*. In the most banal sense, we can catch a glimpse of the *ren's* power when we find ourselves struggling to find a piece of equipment in a hardware store, and only able to describe it to the proprietor in the most general terms. If we knew its name, its *ren*, we could deal with the situation in a portion of the time.

*

The *ka*, which functions via the *ab* and *ren*, then, also has the *khaibit*, which is known as the Shadow and portrayed quite simply as that.

The *khaibit* is that complex of quirks, cruelties, weaknesses and miserable human failings that we all come into this world with, just as surely as we bring the *ka*. Like the *ka*, the *khaibit* can be developed. Often this does nothing more than bring ill to the others for the temporary benefit of the self. But the *khaibit* can also, like Set, teach us where the sun is.

It is in Khemnu, the shadow-place upon the inner planes, where we can learn about the primitive aspects within us. It is through these aspects that we can often touch the greatest sources of personal drive and magical effectiveness. All those 'Cults of the Shadow', those small and secret and (often) sexually-oriented groups and movements which seek to achieve enlightenment and a queer kind of purity by

176

exploring the dark places of the psyche - all these are touching upon the Lovecraftian, subterranean aspects of Khemnu. It is here that we often meet the Dweller on the Threshold, that entity of bestial terror on the inner planes that we all have to confront, and ultimately master, only to find that we have been battling a complex comprised of our own atavistic qualities.

How to deal with the Dweller, or the *khaibit*, has always been a major concern of all those who seek the light.

*

The symbol of the *ba* is:

This is a man-headed bird which inverses the usual symbolism. The *ba* is perhaps more closely related to the ideal of the 'Higher Self' which is part of each individual and yet removed from the world. Crudely speaking, the *ba* inhabits the *ka*, as the *ka* inhabits the *khat*, or physical body. Yet, like the Higher Self, the *ba* is held to belong more truly among the neters.

The *ka* incarnates; it rarely reincarnates. Reincarnation in the popular sense, in which Miss V. dies and then is reborn again with all of Miss V.'s *ka, ba* and *khaibit* occurs less often than imagined. Reincarnation in that sense is not universal. Some *kas* never do anything more than decompose - often within the lifetime of a person who has completely failed to develop any kind of spark.

It is the *ba*, or a portion of it, which is involved in the reincarnation process, learning about the material world by incarnating itself a little bit at a time. Thus several individuals, spread across the world and throughout history, can be linked by the same *ba*, joined to it like puppets on a string. When we fly up to the levels of our own *ba*, we can often glimpse these other aspects, and imagine them to be ourselves in former lives.

In rare cases, amongst what the Tibetans would call the 'twice-born', this may very well be true. But by and large it is not so much that we have former lives, as *other* lives.

After death the whole complex of consciousness finds itself loose within the 'double', the *ka*. In due course the 'Second Death' occurs in which the essence of consciousness, the *ba*, withdraws and enters the clear white light of beyond, leaving the *ka* and the *khaibit* to degenerate in the proper way. However, intense emotions at the point of death can often hold the latter two together, and it is as though the *khaibit* forms a hard carapace which prevents the *ba* from making its departure or its own essence felt. This is what occultists term an 'earth-bound spirit' whose impulses are based upon fear, ignorance, or even lust for power.

*

In almost all ancient cultures there was the stipulation that young people on the edge of puberty (or the Thebes influences in our present scheme) should enter adulthood by means of initiation. The true essence of initiation, however, is not to be found in any occult ceremonial (no matter how awesome this might be) but in the achievement of some difficult but not impossible task, thus exercising the Heart and Will in the truest and fullest of ways.

Certain young we'ebs from Memphis would be sent to Khemnu (often to work on the phobic aspects of their personalities), so that they would also learn to come from 'nothing and nowhere', and take back a spark of a very special kind. The fact that so many of the sacred places in Khemnu were subterranean should give some clues to this. While today we can – *just* - catch a very distant echo of Khemnu's spirit in the proliferation of all those cults of an animist nature, including those ostensibly bizarre sects which focus upon the control of deadly snakes through means of a purified soul.

This is not a path that everyone can follow. But then Khemnu was not a place that everyone wanted to visit.

The actual priests of Khemnu, like the baboons they tended, were often seen as great tricksters. Some of them of course were just crass, and little more than that, but at best the crude and childish and often elaborate jokes played upon the neophytes were intended to invert the normal senses so that they never knew what to expect, and had to start activating those 'learn-and-learn-fast' survival responses within them just to get through the day.

In Khemnu, then, the *khaibit* was most intensely alive. All the darkness within an individual was brought to the surface and examined in Khemnu.

*

It is at the inner levels of Khemnu that we touch upon the adrenal glands, situated at the upper pole of each kidney. We can actually imagine Kha'm-uast using the Set-head of his *uas* wand to gouge a channel down through our *ka*, so that the pituitary, pineal, thyroid, thymus and adrenal glands are actually linked, like seeds within a ploughed furrow, awaiting the waters. Yellowish in colour, the right adrenal gland is triangular, and the left crescent-shaped. Each consists of an outer part (cortex) and an inner part (medulla). They regulate the salt and water metabolism and the neuromuscular function.

This is the gland which is actually responsible for the secretion of epinephrine (also called adrenaline) and norepinephrine, at the behest of the pituitary. Among other things they effect heart rate, blood pressure, and respiration - Heart and Will on another level. They are also responsible for that phenomenon which – literally - causes the hair to stand on end, invariably when the individual feels themself to be in the presence of something unknown and unnameable from dread supernatural realms. In more hirsute epochs, the whole of our body fur would have stood on end.

Just as Khemnu (and Thoth in his role as Initiator) are responsible for helping man to 'wake from sleep' by questioning and overturning his perceptions of reality and the norm, so do these hormones help us awake every morning from a night of unconsciousness. Khemnu was responsible for the Nile's magical current flowing through the Egyptian psyche with appropriate pressure. Whatever 'impurities' were developed during the ostensibly dark practices were filtered clean by those Thoth-developed agencies which paralleled the function of the kidneys.

Just as the occasionally bizarre spirit of Khemnu eventually transferred itself to Alexandria, so today are misfunctions of the adrenal glands dealt with by (among other options) the irradiation, or the complete removal, of the pituitary itself.

179

*

It is through adrenaline, of course, that we discover those unconscious responses known as 'fight or flight', which is an adequate description of man's choices when reduced to this most primitive level. Tied in with the corollary of 'Learn - and learn fast', it is all a question of whether we survive or whether we die. These are the most basic responses needed to cope with and eventually tame an alien and hostile world.

Thoth of Hermopolis is the one who can teach us these lessons. We have already met him in his aspect of the sedate and stately ibis, which feeds in shallow waters, flies in V-formations, nests in flooded woodlands or on islands (such as Khebit), but we have not yet seen him in his other aspect as the baboon.

It is the latter, sometimes known as the Ape of Thoth, which will take us a little closer to Khemnu's spirit.

*

One of the few surviving pieces from the ruins of Hermopolis was a statue depicting a priest with a baboon on his shoulders. When such pieces do manage to survive the millennia we can be sure that they contain messages for us today. The statue itself was mightily battered, worn, but the drawing of it came through with a strange and peculiar detail, as though the original spirit behind the sculptor were saying: 'Remember this if nothing else remember this...'

It was once a piece of European folklore that such apes were carried on the shoulders of fools and simpletons, perhaps in a distant memory of that city where such a thing was seen as a matter of course.

Yet there has always an underlying notion that great wisdom can be expressed by 'playing the fool' in certain circumstances. It is well

180

known that the word 'silly' is derived from *seely*, meaning happy, blessed, or even holy.

To some of the stuffier members of the Egyptian priesthood (and the gods know there were enough of those!) the initiates of Khemnu were an exasperatingly 'silly' lot.

Baboons were, and are, known as 'the dog-faced monkeys'. They are the largest and most intelligent of the Old World monkeys. Notoriously savage if provoked, and extremely powerful out of all proportion to their size, young baboons when tamed can still grow up to make affectionate and trustworthy creatures. The wild baboons sacred to Egypt were a mischievous and restless breed in their natural state, however, travelling in packs of up to 300, keeping close to open country and usually having one big, powerful male as their leader who always fights his way to the overlordship of the tribe. These baboons eat anything, but their favourite food is the scorpion which is sacred to Isis, and closely related to Khebit.

All the qualities of fight-or-flight, and learn and learn fast, can be found within baboons, as well as the prankish, trickster aspects of Hermopolis as a whole. We can discern Khemnu in them either through the wild jape, or the dry *pince sans rire* jokes of Thoth.

And when we laugh until we are sore, we unconsciously hold that area of our body which corresponds with Khemnu.

*

But the baboon holds mysteries beyond simple laughter. The dog-face, the long, large canine teeth, the manlike qualities, all necessarily evoked to the symbolist cast of the Egyptian mind, the air of Anubis, who was also a scavenger, and who also (via his American incarnation as Coyote) manifested humour of the most disconcerting kind - an often extremely black humour.

Not only that but Anubis was extremely closely related to Sothis, the dog-star, which was so closely tied up with Egyptian ideas as to their spiritual origins. Even the Nemyss worn by royalty and seen in most images of Anubis, can be found paralleled by the baboon's long mantle of hair which sometimes splendidly bore the colours of Egypt.

Just as the adrenal glands can often be responsible for virilising manifestations in the female, and sexual precocity in the

181

preadolescent male, so can we clearly discern when the female baboon is in heat.

So the symbol and reality of the baboon necessarily triggered off concepts in the Egyptian initiates which grouped together the concepts of Sirius, sex, our human and animal natures, and now brings into the open the long-standing occult tradition that mankind should never have 'descended into matter' in the first place, but should have continued to exist among the *neters*. It was when elements of mankind's free spirit decided to 'descend' and became involved in the procreative processes of certain ape-like creatures that the 'Fall into Matter' took place.

Whether the Traveller accepts this as initiatic truth, a deep allegory, or just another of the Tall Tales from Hermopolis that all wayfarers get inflicted with, is a matter for his or her own taste. Although if they are wise they will become like the baboon momentarily, and swallow everything, and gain energy from it as they digest.

*

So Khemnu, via the impulses of the baboon but under the decorous eye of the ibis, was the centre for all those impulses and cults which we might now call Priapic. These were not concerned with fertility as such - that was the concern of Abydos and Thebes - but with the intensity of sensual, erotic, and animal experience, and the universal concept of the male and female, positive and negative, locked together in a necessary union as hinted at by the binaries of Nun/Nunet, Amun/Amunet, etc. If the intensity of that union could be fully understood, and prolonged or else developed, then enormous energies can surge through.

In this respect the use of the Hare as a symbol for this particular region within the psyche becomes more apparent. Like the strange frog-gods, the hare with its massive hind legs can swim well, although its sole mode of locomotion is by hopping. It can outrun almost all of its predators not only by speed alone, but by its ability to come to a sudden stop, or turn at a sharp angle.

In some ways we can almost find the spirit of Zen here, for the sudden and unexpected stop and change of direction was a common teaching method in Hermopolis just as it was among the Zen masters.

Prolific breeders, whose defensive methods are always expressed through flight, the bucks or jacks as the males are called, nevertheless fight with tooth and claw amongst their kind in order to have the does, often leaping high in their frenzy - hence the phrase 'mad as a March hare'.

There was also a particular game played by the we'ebs in Hermopolis which was called, in effect, 'Running down the Hare' the object being to actually do that.

The difficulty in catching a hare was not so much in its speed but in those sudden changes of direction. Whenever a hare is about to make such a turn, however, its ears go back, though not all the way back. At this moment the we'eb must simply fling himself down at 90° to the hare's line of flight. He actually has a fifty-fifty chance of being right and catching with relative ease. It is not a matter of rapid analyses, or long internal debates as to terrain or mood of animal, but just a blind and unthinking dive toward the earth. The we'ebs wore simple loin-cloths and nothing else. They often attracted small crowds. They learned very early on that it is sometimes necessary to respond instantly and unconsciously toward given stimulii. Our animal and instinctive responses to the world have just as much a chance of bringing us to life and to light and to love as the finer, 'higher' senses.

*

Apart from the ways they travel through their respective mediums of earth and water, there is another comparison to be made between the hare and the frog in the light of their reproductive processes. Both of them can and do produce large numbers of offspring with great frequency. The huge male frogs of Egypt, between 8 and10 inches in body length, will stand guard over their tadpoles, their heads only just above the water, ready to fend off attack from herons, from Man, and in particular from snakes.

Frogs were probably the first land creatures to use vocal sounds in order to communicate, and the chief purpose of these sounds was to bring the sexes together for breeding. Male frogs had the most developed voice, and the frog's tongue as it captures living prey is a clear symbol of the power of sounds - hence the Thoth connections, in his role as Communicator. The primitive sounds which were uttered as part of a direct adrenaline-response to sudden situations, later developed into words and consciously modulated cries for help. Speech came before thought. The frog-gods within us have come a long way under Thoth's guidance.

*

We cannot consider these frog-gods without looking at the snake-goddesses however.

If the most striking feature of the frog was its limbs, and its slow-blinking eyelids, then the snake is almost the direct opposite in these respects. On the other hand they both have notable tongues. And if the frog would use its tongue to call to Life, then the cobra which symbolised Woman would spit out Death with the same.

Because the female snake can store sperm, she is able to produce offspring several times after a single mating, and the eggs from which the young are hatched link back to the 'cosmic egg' at the centre of Khemnu's fragmented cosmology.

The cobra too, was seen to have two 'eyes' upon its hood and credited with the power of transfixing creatures (such as the hare) with its ruthless, unblinking gaze.

All of these creatures—hare, frog and serpent—are linked with the peculiar atmospheres evoked by those practices now grouped together under the name of witchcraft. They are also connected with those primary senses concerned with our sheer survival:

frog	voice
snake	sight
hare	hearing
baboon	smell

As for touch, that is up to the ibis, to Thoth in his more developed mode. Without touch we could not 'feel' the world. We would not be able to walk, hold things, respond or be able to cope in any way. The physical touch of sex would be without pleasure, mystery, or even import. The emotional sense of being 'touched' by something would make the world a cold place. The mental concepts of minds and ideas touching and mutually stimulating would not exist, and leave us in a fog. The spiritual sense of being touched by something greater than ourselves would be unknown, and leave us rotting in an abyss.

It is in this sense that Thoth ensures we make and maintain links with all of our animal and reptilian aspects, opening all the levels of our primitive responses, harkening right back to the mid-brain again, and its neglected knowledge. The deities of Khemnu may exist within the realms of Infinity, Invisibility, Inertness and Nothing (which can link with the serpent, hare, frog and baboon respectively) but from these primordial, pre-human origins comes the abilities that will enable us to survive within, and ultimately master, the world.

Understandably this is why Thoth is often thought of as being married to Maat: they ensure that the Balance of Nature is maintained, that Man's role toward the animal world is akin to that of the priest carrying the baboon: a support, a relationship built upon respect and joy, and mutual origins. Maat is Thoth's anima: Thoth is the animus of Maat.

Thoth also ensures that when the trickster, prankster aspect of Khemnu breaks through into human consciousness and behaviour, they are in accordance with the natural justice of things.

*

Nothing exists now of any plans as to how Hermopolis may have looked in its heyday. Even the techniques of reaching it on magical levels are entirely a matter of chance, and the Henu Boat can rarely take us into the city itself, the former being too consciously developed as a mental structure. Khemnu runs through our consciousness like the hare, travelling at great speed and apparently with the mad, leaping joy of the witches' dance.

We can create a ritual using four pairs of men and women arranged in the pattern given below, and assuming the ancient names; but the knowledge of what to do then, and how to create the 'Egg of Light' from which the Word is born, is entirely a matter for the frog-like, serpent-like responses of the group as it functions in its most

185

primitive manner, though all the while bound by the watchful and encircling figure of Thoth.

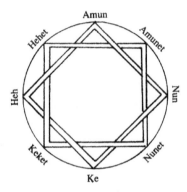

Magic of this sort is instinctive, even if such instincts do become highly developed with use.

As for the individual, he or she can try to enter with Kha'm-uast by stepping through that same figure as though it were a door. They can visualise themself on the back of a hare and riding through it while intoning the actual name of Khemnu. They can assume the god-form of a priest and feel the weight of the baboon on their shoulders, eventually lifting it down to find that its face is strikingly like their own. But in general the spirit of Khemnu will come to them rather than vice-versa. As they go throughout their life they must keep their eyes peeled, their ears open, their tongue silent but their nose twitching. At some moment, at some unpredictable and undefinable time, the wild and primitive spirit of the place will appear within their reach. All they have to do then is make a choice - any choice - and dive toward the earth to grasp it.

Or if they have the nerve they can take a large mirror and set it on their lap in a dark and empty room, sitting legs apart and frog naked with the reflection of the moon's light in the glass, and intoning

Khemnu, Khemnu, Khemnu . . . with a frog-like croaking in the throat, and they will watch while their face changes through its other masks, other *ba* manifestations, back through the ages towards the source.

That, like Khemnu itself, is not for-everyone. So every Traveller should look forward to the day when their own divinely inspired act of folly might appear to offer them the keys to the city.

If the fool who persists in his folly becomes wise, as William Blake once said, then he will come to Khemnu also.